Editor
Sara Connolly

Illustrator
Kevin McCarthy

Cover Artist
Brenda DiAntonis

Managing Editor
Ina Massler Levin, M.A.

Creative Director
Karen J. Goldfluss, M.S. Ed.

Art Production Manager
Kevin Barnes

Art Coordinator
Renée Christine Yates

Imaging
Nathan Rivera
Rosa C. See

Publisher
Mary D. Smith, M.S. Ed.

Author

Debra J. Housel, M.S. Ed.

Teacher Created Resources, Inc.
6421 Industry Way
Westminster, CA 92683
www.teachercreated.com

ISBN: 978-1-4206-8376-9

Reprinted, 2010
Made in U.S.A.

Table of Contents

About This Book

The primary goal of any reading task is comprehension. *Document-Based Questions for Reading Comprehension and Critical Thinking* uses high-interest grade-level nonfiction passages, related documents, and critical thinking assessment practice to help you develop confident readers who can demonstrate their skills on standardized tests. In addition, you will build the comprehension skills necessary for a lifetime of learning.

There are five topic areas with six or seven lessons in each. Each lesson consists of three pages: a passage, a related document, and an assessment practice page containing multiple choice, true-false-explain, and short-answer document-based questions. This gives your students practice in all of the question types used in standardized testing. The students respond to the document-based questions based on the information gleaned from the passage plus its related document. Such questions improve a student's ability to apply prior knowledge, integrate information, and transfer knowledge to a new situation.

Readability

These passages have a 6.0–6.9 reading level based on the Flesch-Kincaid Readability Formula. This formula, built into *Microsoft® Word™*, determines readability by calculating the number of words, syllables, and sentences. Average readability was determined for each of the five topic areas. The topics are presented in order of increasing difficulty.

The documents are not leveled. Many of them are historical pieces and therefore replicated with the exact wording. Some terminology may be challenging, but your students can handle difficult words within the context given.

Preparing Students to Read Nonfiction Text

One of the best ways to prepare students to read expository text is to read a short selection aloud to them daily. Reading expository text aloud is critical to developing your students' ability to read it themselves. Since making predictions is another way to make students tap into their prior knowledge, read the beginning of a passage, then stop, and ask them to predict what might occur next. Do this at several points throughout your reading of the text. By doing this, over time you will find that your students' ability to make accurate predictions increases.

Your questions will help students, especially struggling readers, to focus on what's important in a text. Also, remember the significance of wait time. Research has shown that the amount of time an educator waits for a student to answer after posing a question has a critical effect on learning. So after you ask a student a question, silently count to five (ten if you have a student who really struggles to put his or her thoughts into words) before giving any additional prompts or redirecting the question to another student.

Talking about nonfiction concepts is also important. Remember, however, that discussion can never replace reading aloud because people rarely speak using the vocabulary and complex sentence structures of written language.

Applying Bloom's Taxonomy

The questions on the assessment practice pages in *Document-Based Questions for Reading Comprehension and Critical Thinking* assess all levels of learning in Bloom's Taxonomy. Benjamin Bloom devised this six-level classification system for comprehension questions. The questions on each assessment practice passage are always presented in this order. They progress from easiest to most challenging.

- **Level 1: Knowledge**—Students recall information or can find requested information in an article. They recognize dates, events, places, people, and main ideas.
- **Level 2: Comprehension**—Students understand information. This means that they can find information that is stated in a different way than the question. It also means students can rephrase or restate information in their own words.
- **Level 3: Application**—Students apply their knowledge to a specific situation. They may be asked to do something new with the knowledge.
- **Level 4: Analysis**—Students break things into their component parts and examine those parts. They notice patterns in information.
- **Level 5: Synthesis**—Students do something new with the information. They integrate knowledge and create new ideas. They generalize, predict, plan, and draw conclusions.
- **Level 6: Evaluation**—Students make judgments and assess value. They form an opinion and defend it. They can also understand another person's viewpoint.

These skills are essential to keep in mind when teaching comprehension to assure that your students practice the higher levels of thinking. Use this classification to form your own questions whenever your students read or listen to material.

Assessment Practice Pages

Teach your students to read the passage and its related document before answering any of the questions on the assessment practice page. Armed with this information, your students can more rapidly and accurately answer each question.

Multiple Choice Questions

The first three questions are multiple choice. Based solely on the information given in the passage, they cover the knowledge, comprehension, and application levels of Bloom's taxonomy.

For these questions, demonstrate your own thought process by doing a "think aloud" to figure out an answer. Tell your students your thoughts as they come to you. For example, suppose the question was: "In Yellowstone National Park, grizzly bears (a) do tricks, (b) roam free, (c) stay in cages, or (d) get caught in traps."

Tell the students all your thoughts as they occur to you:

"Well, the grizzly bears living in Yellowstone National Park are wild bears. So of course they don't do tricks. And it didn't mention that they stay in cages. They probably only do that in zoos or circuses. So I'll get rid of choices A and C. That leaves me with 'roam free' or 'get caught in traps.' Let me look back at the passage and see what it says about traps." (Refer back to article.)

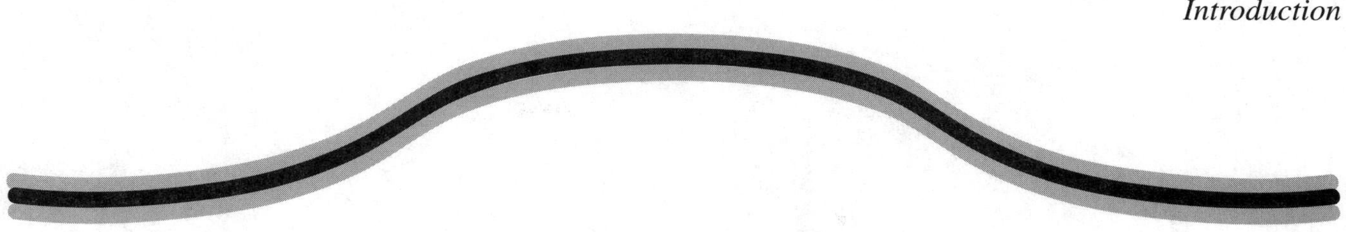

Applying Bloom's Taxonomy

Multiple Choice Questions *(cont.)*

"I don't see anything about traps in the passage. And I did see that it says that in Yellowstone National Park the bears are protected and their population is increasing. That means they're safe from traps, which are dangerous. So I'm going to select (b)—roam free."

True/False—Explain Questions

The fourth question is true-false-explain. It tests the analysis level of Bloom's taxonomy. This question may require students to use information from both the passage and the document to generate an answer. Just a one- or two-sentence response is required. To respond correctly, the student must not only distinguish facts from falsehoods but also explain them. This requires logical reasoning and analytical thinking. They cannot receive full credit without an adequate explanation. You must demonstrate how to write a good explanation. For example, in response to the statement: "Thomas Jefferson wrote the Gettysburg Address," the students could write, "False. Abraham Lincoln wrote the Gettysburg Address" OR "False. Thomas Jefferson wrote the Declaration of Independence." Either answer is acceptable and worth full credit.

When the statement is clearly true, the student must state that and add information. For example, in response to the statement: "Early pioneers in the Midwest had to cope with grasshopper plagues," the students should write, "True. The grasshoppers destroyed crops and even damaged buildings."

Make sure that your students know that sometimes both true and false responses can be correct. For example, in an article about rescuing Jewish children from the Warsaw Ghetto, it states how hard it was to convince the parents to let the rescue organization take away their children. It also details the methods used to get the kids past the guards (crawling through sewers, sedated babies in toolboxes). In response to the question, "During the rescue operation, the most difficult part was getting the parents to release their kids to the rescuers," some students may respond "True. Many parents did not want to let their children go. They were not sure that the children were in danger and thought that they could protect them." But others may say, "False. The hardest part was getting the kids out of the Ghetto without the Gestapo discovering what was going on."

Either response is worth full credit because it is adequately defended. This promotes critical thinking since the students must digest the information in order to take a stance.

Document-Based Questions

The remaining questions require the students to integrate the information provided in the passage with the information shown in the document. You must guide your students in understanding and responding to the document-based questions. Again, the best way to teach such skills is to demonstrate the formulation of an answer through a think aloud.

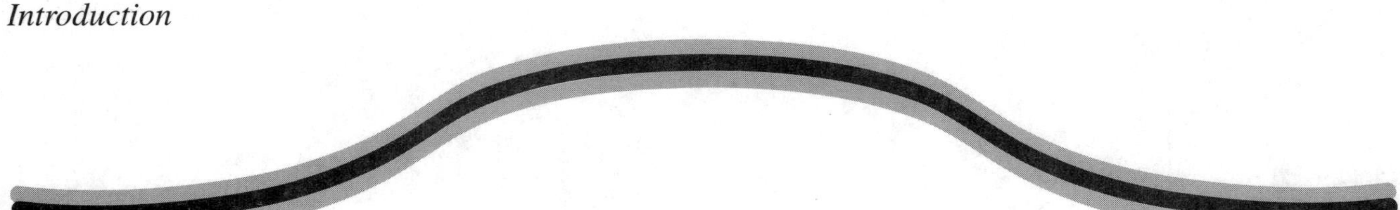

Applying Bloom's Taxonomy

Short-Answer Questions

The fifth and sixth questions test the synthesis and evaluative levels of Bloom's taxonomy. Synthesis questions make your students draw conclusions based on information gleaned from both the passage and its document. Their respond requires only a few sentences. Show your students how to restate the words from the question to formulate a cogent response. For example, in response to "Why were some people against the building of the Hoover Dam?" the students could write, "Some people were against the building of the Hoover Dam because it backed up a river, forming a huge lake. Historical Native American sites were flooded and animals' homes destroyed."

The final short answer question will be evaluative—the highest level of Bloom's taxonomy. This means that it is an opinion statement with no right answer. Evaluative questions demand the highest thinking and logical reasoning skills. The child must take a stance and defend it. Although there is no correct response, it is critical that the students support their opinions using facts and logic. Show them a format for the defense—by stating their opinion followed by the word "because" and a reason. For example, have a student respond to this question "Do you think that whales should be kept in aquariums and sea parks for people to enjoy?" The student may respond, "I do not think that whales should be kept at sea parks because they are wild animals and don't want to be there. They want to be free in the ocean." Do not award full credit unless the student adequately supports his or her opinion.

Sample defenses are given for the evaluative questions, but students may present other valid opinions as well. Also, it would be most effective if you used the defenses written by the students themselves. Thus, before passing back the practice papers, make note of two children who had opposing opinions. Then, during the wrap-up discussion, call on each of these students to read his or her defense to the class. If all the children had the same conclusion, give the opposing opinion from the answer key to show them both sides of the issue. When it's obvious that a topic has generated strong opinions in your students, you can encourage your class to debate.

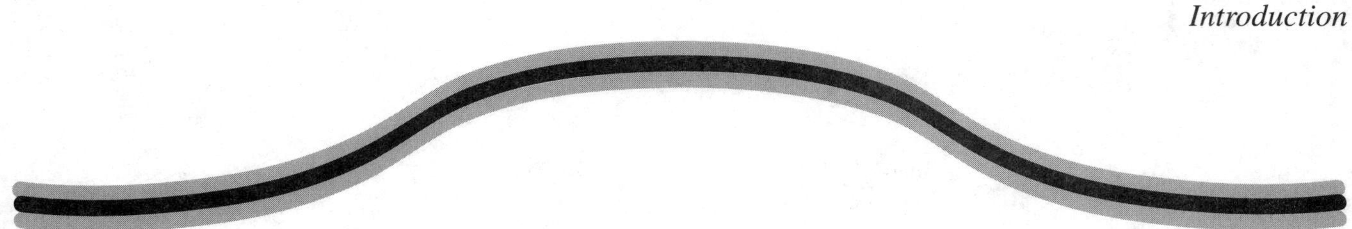

Practice Suggestions

Read aloud the first passage in each of the five topic areas and do its related questions with the whole class. Such group practice is essential. The more your students practice, the more competent and confident they will become. Plan to have your class do every exercise in the *Document-Based Questions for Reading Comprehension and Critical Thinking*. The activities are time-efficient so that your students can practice each week. To yield the best results, practice must begin at the start of the school year.

If you have some students who cannot read the articles independently, allow them to read with a partner, then work through the comprehension questions alone. Eventually all students must practice reading and answering the questions independently. Move to this stage as soon as possible. For the most effective practice sessions, follow these steps:

1. Have students read the text silently and answer the questions.
2. Have students exchange papers to correct each other's multiple choice section.
3. Collect all the papers to score the short answer questions.
4. Return the papers to their owners and discuss how the students determined their answers.
5. Refer to the exact wording in the passage.
6. Point out how students had to use their background knowledge to answer certain questions.
7. Discuss the document-based questions thoroughly. Do think-alouds to show how you integrated information from the passage and the document to formulate your response.
8. Discuss how a child should defend his or her stance in an evaluative short-answer question.

Scoring the Assessment Practice Passages

To generate a numeric score, follow these guidelines:

Multiple Choice Questions (3)	12 points each		36 points
True/False—Explain Question (1)	16 points		16 points
Short-Answer Questions (2)	24 points each		48 points
		Total	100 points

Standardized Test Success

A key objective of *Document-Based Questions for Reading Comprehension and Critical Thinking* is to prepare your students to get the best possible scores on standardized tests. You may want to practice environmental conditions throughout the year in order to get your students used to the testing environment. For example, if your students' desks are usually together, have students move them apart whenever you practice so it won't feel strange on the test day.

A student's ability to do well on traditional standardized tests on comprehension requires these good test-taking skills. Thus, every student in your class needs instruction in test-taking skills. Even fluent readers and logical thinkers will perform better on standardized tests if you provide instruction in these areas:

- Understanding the question: Teach students to break down the question to figure out what is really being asked of them. This book will prepare them for the kinds of questions they will encounter on standardized tests.
- Concentrating on what the text says: Show students how to restrict their response to just what is asked. When you go over the practice pages, ask your students to show where they found the correct response or inference in the text.
- Ruling out distracters in multiple choice answers: Teach students to look for the key words in a question and look for those specific words to find the information in the text. They also need to know that they may have to look for synonyms for the key words.
- Maintaining concentration: Use classroom time to practice this in advance. Reward students for maintaining concentration. Explain to them the purpose of this practice and the reason why concentration is so essential.

Students will need to use test-taking skills and strategies throughout their lives. The exercises in *Document-Based Questions for Reading Comprehension and Critical Thinking* will guide your students to become better readers and test-takers. After practicing the exercises in this book, you will be pleased with your students' comprehension performance, not only on standardized tests, but with any expository text they encounter—within the classroom and beyond its walls.

Look Out Below! Here Comes the Snow

Ski Safety Tips

Heaven's Valley Ski Resort Safety Brochure—Avalanche Survival Tips

Here at Heaven's Valley Ski Resort, we take precautions to ensure your safety and prevent avalanches. Whenever you are on the mountain, you must wear the rescue beacon given to you at check-in. Violators of this policy will have their lift pass privileges revoked.

We have a daily patrol that monitors the mountain ridges. They report to a helicopter crew that drops explosives just after daybreak. This creates controlled slides to prevent more major ones. However, snow sports involve risk, and we cannot control nature. So, if an avalanche begins while you are on the mountain, here's what to do:

1. **Get Out of the Way!** Get off the ski run and move perpendicular to the slide to get into the trees. Even if the snow overtakes you there, it will be moving more slowly. The trees will also trap much of the snow.
2. **Take Shelter!** Get off the ski run and get under a rock shelf perpendicular to the slide. Even if the snow buries the shelf, the area beneath it will have an air pocket. This will let you breathe until you or rescuers can dig you out.

3. **Abandon Your Equipment!** Once you're caught in the sliding snow, kick off your skis or snowboard or snowshoes. Drop your poles. Otherwise your equipment will cause you to twist and probably break a bone.
4. **Grab an Anchor!** If you can, grab a tree and hold on tight. That way, when the snow stops, you'll know where the surface is—up the tree. People trapped under the snow can get confused about which way to dig and waste precious time digging themselves deeper into the snow!
5. **Stay on Top of the Snow!** If you're caught in the open in the fastest moving snow, use your arms and legs to "swim." Make strong strokes as if you're coming up from a dive. When the snow stops, the closer to the surface you are, the better your chances of survival.
6. **Move Around!** As the snow begins to slow down, move your arms and legs as much as possible. This will create a small air pocket for you once the slide stops.
7. **Stay Calm!** If the sliding stops but you can't move, don't waste energy struggling. You must stay calm or you will use up your air too rapidly.
8. **Turn on Your Rescue Beacon!** That's why we provide it. By following its signal, we can find you fast.

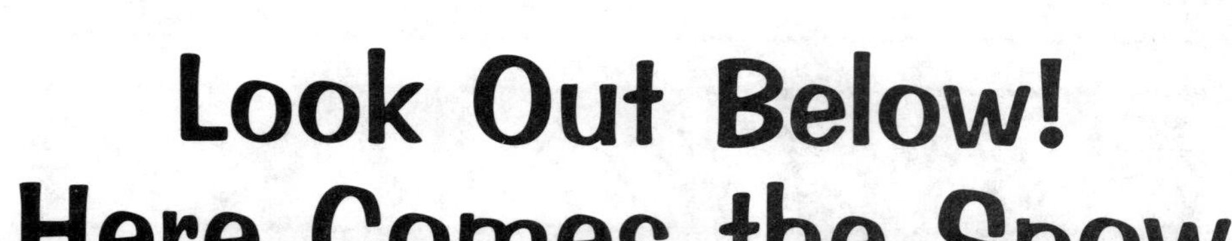

Look Out Below! Here Comes the Snow

1. Most avalanches begin from

a. loud noises.

b. the weight of heavy snow.

c. earthquakes.

d. bombs.

2. Many ski trails are actually

a. avalanche-proof.

b. designed to run perpendicular to. typical avalanche paths.

c. closed during avalanche season.

d. avalanche paths.

3. What made using avalanches to kill enemy troops in the Alps dangerous to the men starting the slide?

a. An avalanche cannot be controlled, so it might bury the army that started it.

b. It gave away the location of the army starting the slide to the enemy.

c. It was an ineffective way to kill lots of soldiers.

d. It would infuriate the surviving troops into using nuclear weapons.

4. The best thing to do if you see an avalanche coming toward you is to move as fast as you can in a perpendicular direction to the avalanche's path. True or False? Explain.

____

____

____

5. Could the survival information given in the Heaven's Valley Ski Resort Safety Brochure have saved the lives of many people in the Yungay, Peru, avalanche?

____

____

____

____

____

6. Do you think it's fair for a ski resort's management to take away a patron's lift pass (which the person paid for) if that person refuses to wear a rescue beacon on the mountain? Defend your stance.

____

____

____

____

____

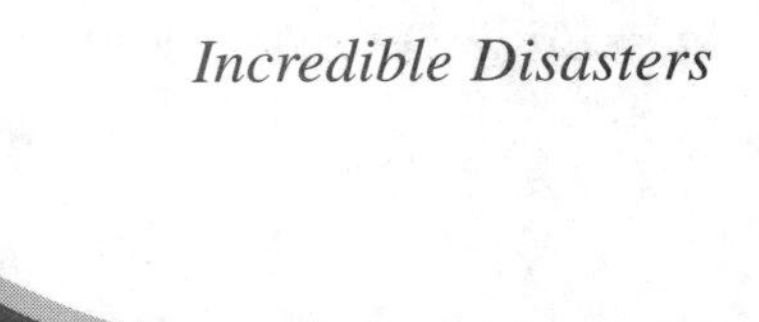

Horror in Halifax

In 1917 the nations of Europe were fighting World War I. Canada had close ties to Great Britain. So it was on the side of the Allies. The Canadians sent them ships filled with weapons, ammunition, and explosives. These munitions were shipped from Halifax, a city in Nova Scotia. The city was ready to defend itself against a German airship or submarine attack. But there was no way to prepare for the kind of disaster that destroyed it.

Halifax Harbor lay at the end of a long, thin channel called the narrows. On the morning of December 6, 1917, the *Mont Blanc* steamed up the narrow channel toward the open sea. It carried 9,000 gallons of benzol, a highly flammable fluid, and 7,000 tons of TNT (explosives). Heading toward this ship was the *Imo*. This empty cargo ship was coming to pick up munitions.

Although the *Imo* blew its whistle to indicate that it saw the *Mont Blanc*, it did not alter its course. Instead it plowed straight into the ship! The benzol spilled down into the *Mont Blanc*'s hold and caught fire. At first the crew tried to fight the blaze to keep it from reaching the TNT. But the captain gave orders to abandon ship. The crew leapt into rowboats, raced to shore, and ran as fast as they could. The nearby tugboat *Stella Maris* turned its fire hose on the burning ship, but the water didn't really help.

The British warship *High Flyer* had intended to escort the *Mont Blanc* across the Atlantic. Its captain ordered his men to sink the vessel. They had just climbed onto its deck when the *Mont Blanc* detonated. The *Imo* was blown out of the water and onto the shore! The blast was heard six miles away. It was the largest man-made explosion until the first atomic bomb test 28 years later.

But the worst was still to come. The explosion caused a chain reaction in the munitions stacked on the docks waiting to be loaded onto ships. Homes, factories, and schools vanished. About 325 acres of buildings were flattened. A local Native American village and everyone in it disappeared without a trace. Huge waves caused by the blast washed over the city and dragged people out to sea.

No one knows the exact death toll, but at least 2,000 people died and many more were hurt. At least 6,000 were left homeless. But it could have been even worse. Just moments before he died, a telegrapher sent a message. It stated that a ship was ablaze and drifting toward the munitions. This sent rescuers rushing to the area with medical supplies, food, and clothing.

Like a phoenix, the city of Halifax rose quickly from its ashes. It soon became a busy port once more. During World War II, Halifax was the main port in North America for ships carrying food and war supplies to the Allies in Europe.

Horror in Halifax

December 8, 1917

Dear Mother,

I want to assure you of my safety. I am alive on Prince Edward Island in Canada. By now you will have read in the papers of the great tragedy that befell my ship and crew and the harbor at Halifax. My only injury is my hearing. It's dulled considerably. I still cannot believe that I am alive to tell about it.

We were fully loaded with benzol and TNT as we steamed up the Narrows. The Imo gave us confusing signals. Although our good Captain Le Médec tried to veer away, we had no time or space. The Imo ran into us head on! My mates and I fought the resulting fire as best we could. We knew that if it reached the TNT we were dead men. We made no headway against the blaze, so the captain gave orders to abandon ship. I was relieved! We leaped into lifeboats and rowed for shore as if the devil were after us. Our ship drifted toward the docks. A big crowd had gathered onshore to watch the blaze. The moment we touched shore, we jumped from our boat and shouted at them to run for their lives. But most of them didn't understand French. They looked at us like we were crazy! As we ran through the streets, we screamed at every person we saw to run. But it did no good. Everyone was rushing toward the docks. Poor fools.

My heart pounded and my lungs felt on fire, but I kept running. Some of my mates fell behind, and I yelled at them to hurry up. We had just reached the edge of town when we heard a sound I can't even describe. It knocked me flat on my face. I think I passed out. The next thing I knew, Pierre was slapping me and telling me to get up. I stumbled to my feet and kept moving away from the blast. There were more explosions, although none so loud as the first. I thought my life was over. At last we reached some woods and sank down into the snow shaking and weeping.

We kept walking until we reached another town. We soon found out that many people blamed us for abandoning our burning ship. But it was the Imo's fault! And there was no way we could've kept the disaster from occurring. So I am not ashamed to be alive. But I am using a false name to apply to ships in the hopes of returning to France. I do not relish boarding a ship again, but of course there is no other way to get home. And I don't want to stay here for fear my true identity will be discovered. I will be home as soon as I join another ship's crew. I am not eager for the trip across the sea with the German U-boats determined to sink all vessels.

There have been no reports of looting as often happens after a disaster. The people here and in the States have worked together to help the survivors. I love you, Mother. Pray for me as I do for you.

Your son,

Luc

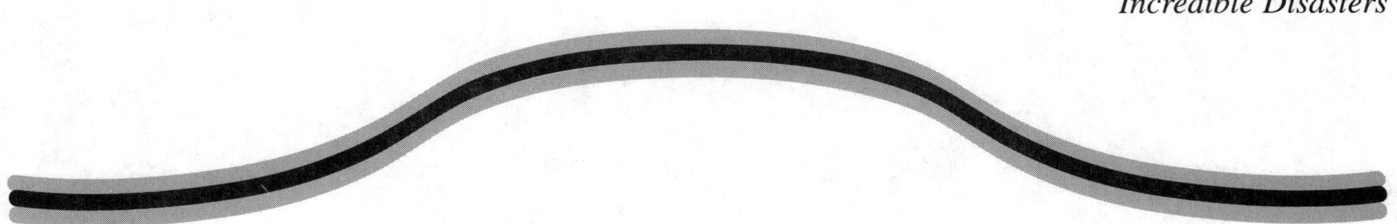

Horror in Halifax

1. Which ship rammed another one in the Narrows?
   a. the
   b. the
   c. the
   d. the
2. The chain reaction in the munitions was most like a
   a. marshmallow roasting over a campfire.
   b. row of dominoes falling down.
   c. lot of cars stuck in a traffic jam.
   d. cake rising in an oven.
3. Why did the British captain order his crew to sink the ?
   a. He was really a German spy who wanted to wreck the ship.
   b. He wanted to get insurance money for the .
   c. He thought that sinking the ship would stop the blaze.
   d. He hoped that he and his men would become internationally famous.
4. People ran to the harbor because they wanted to witness the largest manmade explosion. True or False? Explain.

   ____

   ____

   ____

5. Why is the letter writer applying for work using a false name?

   ____

   ____

   ____

   ____

   ____

6. Did the 's crew take the right action when they abandoned their ship? Defend your stance.

   ____

   ____

   ____

   ____

   ____

The *Hindenburg* Tragedy

Airships are also called blimps. They float because they are filled with a gas that's lighter than air. In the early part of the 20th century it seemed as if blimps would own the skies. Why? In 1900 a German named Ferdinand von Zeppelin had created an airship. It had a rigid frame. It held individual hydrogen gas cells. His first design flew 17 miles per hour (27 km/h). He made improvements in his next designs. Then, in 1909 he created the first airline for passengers. He named it DELAG.

Zeppelin's passenger airship *Hindenburg* (LZ-129) was the biggest aircraft to ever fly. She was an engineering marvel. Each of the 25 two-bed cabins had heat as well as hot and cold running water. There was a spacious dining room, a lounge, and an observation room lined with windows. The ship also had a smoking room. Some people questioned the wisdom of having it. After all, hydrogen is flammable. But precautions were taken. Double doors kept the smoke inside. And the only lighter on board the ship was fastened to a chain attached to the room's wall.

In May 1936 the *Hindenburg* offered the first transatlantic air service. For one year she carried hundreds of passengers and flew thousands of miles with a perfect safety record. Then she met with a terrible disaster on May 6, 1937. It happened at Naval Air Station Lakehurst in New Jersey. The airship carried 36 passengers and 61 crew members.

During the landing, at an altitude of about 200 feet, a fire started near the *Hindenburg*'s stern (end). No one knows for sure what caused it. In less than 35 seconds, the airship fell to the ground completely engulfed by flames. Of those aboard, just 12 passengers and 37 crew survived. And most of those were injured. Every year on the fateful date a memorial service is held in Lakehurst at 7:25 P.M. to honor the victims.

The use of airships came to an abrupt halt after the disaster. People were afraid to board one. From then on, planes set the standard for passenger flights. Yet the disaster would not have occurred had the *Hindenburg* been filled with helium. In fact, its designers had urged its use. Unlike hydrogen, helium is inert. That means that it does not react with other substances. It would never explode or cause a fire.

Helium was available in the United States, but the nation's leaders refused to sell it to Nazi Germany. They believed that Adolf Hitler, its ruler, might use airships as military weapons.

The *Hindenburg* Tragedy

One of history's most famous radio broadcasts occurred during the tragic demise. Herbert Morrison, a correspondent with Chicago's WLS, and his sound engineer, Charlie Nehlson, witnessed the event and were on the air as it happened. This is the transcript of his radio broadcast:

"The ship is riding majestically toward us like some great feather, riding as though it was mighty good, mighty proud of the place it's playing in the world's aviation. The ship is no doubt bustling with activity as we can see; orders are shouted to the crew, the passengers probably lining the windows looking down at the field ahead of them, getting their glimpse of the mooring mast.

There are a number of important persons on board, and no doubt the new commander, Captain Max Pruss, is thrilled, too, for this is his great moment, the first time he's commanded the Hindenburg. On previous flights, he acted as Chief Officer under Captain Lehmann.

It's practically standing still now. They've dropped ropes out of the nose of the ship, and it's been taken a hold of down on the field by a number of men. It's starting to rain again; the rain had slacked up a little bit. The back motors of the ship are just holding it, just enough to keep it from . . . It burst into flames! Get out of the way! Get out of the way! Get this, Charlie! Get this, Charlie! It's fire and it's crashing! It's crashing terrible! Oh, my! Get out of the way, please! It's burning, bursting into flames and is falling on the mooring mast, and all the folks agree that this is terrible. This is the worst of the worst catastrophes in the world! Oh, it's crashing . . . oh, four or five hundred feet into the sky, and it's a terrific crash, ladies and gentlemen. There's smoke, and there's flames, now, and the frame is crashing to the ground, not quite to the mooring mast . . . Oh, the humanity, and all the passengers screaming around here!

I told you . . .I can't even talk to people . . . around there. It's—I can't talk, ladies and gentlemen. Honest, it's just laying there, a mass of smoking wreckage, and everybody can hardly breathe and talk . . . I, I'm sorry. Honest, I can hardly breathe. I'm going to step inside where I cannot see it. Charlie, that's terrible. I—Listen folks, I'm going to have to stop for a minute, because I've lost my voice . . . This is the worst thing I've ever witnessed."

Navy Lakehurst Historical Society. "Tragedy at Lakehurst."
http://www.nlhs.com/tragedy.htm

The *Hindenburg* Tragedy

1. The last name of the person who built the first airship is
   - a. Lakehurst.
   - b. Delag.
   - c. von Zeppelin.
   - d. Hindenburg.
2. The tragedy was caused by
   - a. someone smoking onboard the blimp.
   - b. the ground crew's error.
   - c. sabotage by an airplane manufacturer.
   - d. an undetermined event.
3. Airships carried passengers for
   - a. 1 year.
   - b. 17 years.
   - c. 28 years.
   - d. 37 years.
4. It was immediately clear to the radio correspondent Herbert Morrison what caused the fire. True or False? Explain.

   ____

   ____

   ____

5. Describe the emotions of Herbert Morrison before, during, and after the accident.

   ____

   ____

   ____

   ____

   ____

6. Did American leaders make the right decision by refusing to sell helium to Nazi Germany? Defend your stance.

   ____

   ____

   ____

   ____

   ____

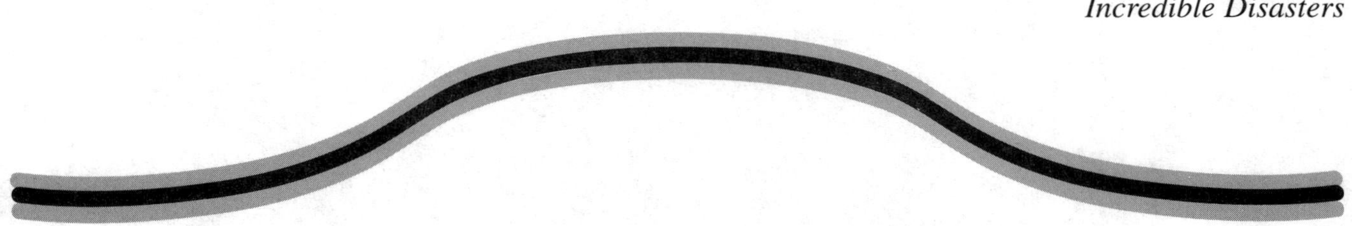

Space Shuttle Disasters

The space shuttle rose from its launch pad at 11:38 A.M. on January 28, 1986. By 11:40 A.M. it no longer existed. All seven members of the crew died about 60 seconds after liftoff. Hundreds of people, including the crew's families and friends, saw the shuttle blow up nine miles above them. Millions more saw it replayed on television.

It was 's tenth flight. On board was the first teacher ever chosen to go into space. Christa McAuliffe taught high school social studies. She planned to keep a journal and teach lessons from space. She had been the unanimous choice of NASA. The committee considered her a gifted teacher who had a special ability to communicate with students.

McAuliffe was not the first civilian in the space shuttle. Representatives of the companies launching payloads and U.S. Congress members had gone on prior missions. The American people had come to take space flight, already in existence for over 20 years, as a routine matter.

The disaster caused shock, grief, and disbelief. A gas leak from a faulty seal in a solid-fuel booster rocket caused the blast. The NASA program recovered. In September 1988 the space shuttle launched successfully.

As the years passed, people began to take space travel for granted once more. But then, on February 1, 2003, disaster struck again. The oldest shuttle in the fleet, , had had an uneventful flight. But as it reentered Earth's atmosphere, it blew up over Texas. The tragedy occurred just 16 minutes before it was to land. Every member of the seven-person crew died.

A piece of foam insulation caused this accident. It broke off from the shuttle's external fuel tank and hit the left wing. This happened just after liftoff. It made a hole in the wing's heat-resistant panels. These panels shield the wings from high temperatures during reentry. The hole let hot air enter the wing and weaken it. The wing fell apart, and so did the shuttle.

This time there was no question about the space shuttle program's continuation. It had to go on. The International Space Station was only partially built. But astronauts were already living aboard it. Only space shuttles could dock there. They had to bring supplies and pick up the people. So NASA improved its fleet. Then the space shuttle lifted off in July 2005.

Space Shuttle Disasters

January 30, 1986

MCAULIFFE, S. Christa. Age 37. Suddenly on January 28 in Cape Canaveral, Florida. Survived by Steven, her husband of 16 years, and two children, Scott and Caroline; her parents, Edward and Grace Corrigan, brothers Christopher and Stephen Corrigan, sisters Lisa Bristol and Betsy Corrigan; and many dear friends. Christa taught for three years at Concord High School. She was selected from over 11,500 applicants to be the first teacher in space. Internment at Calvary Cemetery, Concord, New Hampshire.

Space Shuttle Disasters

1. The space shuttle *Challenger* was destroyed by
   a. a faulty seal in a booster rocket.
   b. high temperatures during reentry into Earth's atmosphere.
   c. a damaged wing.
   d. a failure of its heat-resistant panels.
2. Unlike the *Challenger* disaster, the *Columbia* disaster
   a. occurred just after liftoff.
   b. did not kill the entire crew.
   c. did not completely destroy the space shuttle
   d. occurred just before landing.
3. The amount of time that passed between the two space shuttle disasters was
   a. 7 years.
   b. 10 years.
   c. 17 years.
   d. 27 years.
4. Christa McAuliffe was chosen by NASA because she had so many years of teaching experience. True or False? Explain.

   ____

5. How do you think Christa McAuliffe felt when she was chosen to be the first teacher in space? Use information from her obituary in your response.

   ____

6. Should NASA allow civilians to fly on the space shuttles? Defend your stance.

   ____

Waves that Shook the Planet: The 2004 Tsunami

A massive tsunami killed nearly 300,000 people in Southeast Asia on December 26, 2004. The giant waves were the result of a strong earthquake below the Indian Ocean. It was more powerful than all of the world's earthquakes since 1998 combined! Scientists believe that it had the power of 23,000 atom bombs. It actually made Earth wobble on its axis and spin slightly faster. The quake occurred about 8:00 A.M. just 155 miles off the shore of Sumatra. It shook for four minutes. Those four minutes caused the worst tsunami of modern times.

Most tsunamis occur in the Pacific Ocean. They are usually the result of an undersea earthquake in shallow water. But landslides that change the sea floor or volcanic eruptions can also cause them. As the seabed is heaved upward, it displaces huge amounts of water. This forms the waves of a tsunami. Scientists know that warning people to flee is the only course of action once one forms. They have placed sensors on the ocean floor to monitor the depth of the water above. These sensors send data to a buoy. The buoy sends the information to satellite. From there it is beamed to the Pacific Tsunami Warning Center in Hawaii. But there are none of these sensors in the Indian Ocean! This is tragic, because the people in Sumatra and other parts of Indonesia had no warning.

Fifteen minutes after the quake, the first giant wave reached northern Sumatra. It crashed onto shore, drowning everything in its path. Then it receded, dragging the dead and the living out to sea. Rescuers rushed to the beach to look for survivors. Suddenly another huge wall of water appeared. It raced toward them at over 500 miles an hour. No one could outrun it. Over the next seven hours several more giant waves hit the coast. They were unpredictable and followed no pattern. They battered 12 nations.

Sumatra suffered the worst hit. Whole villages and everyone in them vanished. Afterwards people were buried in mass graves. Food and water were in short supply. The whole region was declared a disaster area. It took years for the villages to be rebuilt. And many people were too afraid to go back. They refuse to live near a coast ever again. And who can blame them?

Waves that Shook the Planet: The 2004 Tsunami

Deadliest Tsunamis in Recorded History in Chronological Order

Date	Place(s) Hit & Wave Origin	Lives Lost	Cause
1755	Lisbon, Portugal Atlantic Ocean	100,000	earthquake
1782	islands South China Sea	40,000	earthquake
1883	Java and Sumatra, Indonesia Indian Ocean	36,000	volcanic eruption on a nearby island
1896	Sanriku, Japan Pacific Ocean	27,000	earthquake
1908	Messina, Italy Mediterranean Sea	70,000	earthquake
1946	Hilo, Hawaii and Japan Pacific Ocean	6,000	earthquake off Chile's coast
2004	Java and Sumatra, Indonesia, India, and east coast of Africa Indian Ocean	283,100	earthquake

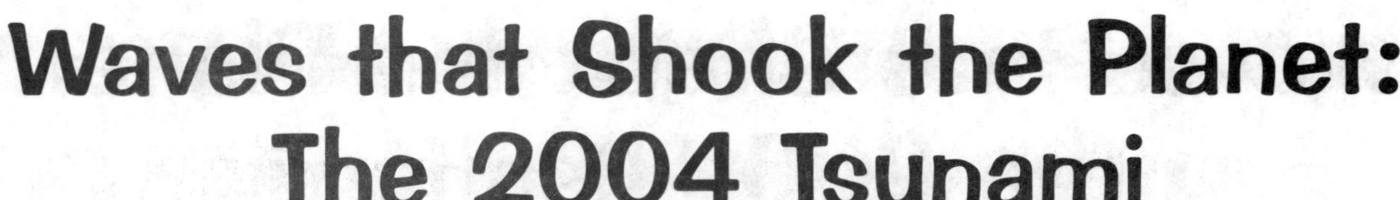

Waves that Shook the Planet: The 2004 Tsunami

1. The 2004 tsunami damaged 12 nations with

a. earthquakes.
b. volcanic eruptions.
c. high winds.
d. tall, fast-moving ocean waves.

2. Tsunamis are usually the result of

a. hurricanes.
b. flooding.
c. earthquakes.
d. avalanches.

3. Tsunami sensors have been placed throughout the

a. Atlantic Ocean.
b. Pacific Ocean.
c. Arctic Ocean.
d. Indian Ocean.

4. The people in Sumatra died because they had no idea that the tsunami was on its way. True or false? Explain.

____

____

____

5. Based on the information given in the table, what was the second-worst tsunami in recorded history and was its cause the same as the tsunami of 2004?

____

____

____

____

____

6. After the 1883 tsunami, parts of Java were considered too dangerous to be resettled and became parkland. Should the Indonesian government forbid people to live in the coastal areas of Java and Sumatra? Defend your stance.

____

____

____

____

____

Prison Reform at Eastern State Penitentiary

Prior to 1829 all prisoners, including children, were put into one large cell and left to fight over food, water, and blankets. Then the Philadelphia Society for Alleviating the Miseries of Public Prisons formed the world's first prison reform group. It said that such conditions were wrong. Most members were Quakers. They felt that given time to reflect on and regret their crimes, convicts could become good citizens. The Society thought that this would happen through solitary confinement. They offered a $100 prize for the best design for Eastern State Penitentiary. The first prison ever built to reform criminals would stand 1.5 miles outside the city of Philadelphia. (Now it is in the midst of the city.)

John Haviland won. He designed the outside of the prison to look like a fortress. The inside layout had a hub and spokes like a wheel. The hub was the center and each cell block a spoke. A guard could stand in the center and look down every cell block. Each cell had a small, high skylight for natural lighting and two doors. One led into a tiny walled exercise area. The other opened into the cell block. Each cell was 8 feet by 12 feet. It held a bed, a workbench, and a toilet flushed with water once a day. There was central heating, too. At that time even the U.S. president didn't have a toilet or central heating. The Society wanted the prisoners treated well.

Every three weeks each inmate took a bath. When they left their cells, a bag was put over their heads. This way they couldn't see the prison's layout and make escape plans. A prisoner could only speak to the guards or the chaplain. He never saw another inmate. He stood in silence at his workbench doing a trade a guard had taught him. The men dyed cloth, wove fabric, made shoes, and caned chairs. The best trade was learning to garden. It meant working in the greenhouse.

The inmates had two short exercise breaks in an outside walled area each day and a Bible—which most of them didn't know how to read. They had no visitors, newspapers, or other reading material. An inmate could not read or pray aloud, sing, or even speak within his cell. Breaking the silence resulted in bread-and-water meals. The isolation and silence made many lose their minds. Now we know that solitary confinement is the most dreaded prison punishment.

At the time it was built in 1829, Eastern State Penitentiary was the largest building in the United States. Called the Pennsylvania System, more than 300 prisons around the world were modeled after it. But solitary confinement was costly. Taxpayers demanded that more people be housed in the same building. So half of all the cell blocks had a second story added. The inmates on the upper story did not get an outdoor exercise area.

In 1913 the silence ended, and inmates started having cellmates. By 1940 the prisoners did the prison's maintenance to keep costs down. This led to escape attempts. After a riot in 1961, the prison started shutting down. The last prisoner left in 1971. Today it is a National Historic Landmark open to visitors. Partially in ruins, the prison is being restored.

Prison Reform at Eastern State Penitentiary

Meeting Minutes of the Philadelphia Society for Alleviating the Miseries of Public Prisons

Benjamin Franklin called the first meeting of the Philadelphia Society for Alleviating the Miseries of Public Prisons to order at 6:30 p.m. on January 12, 1787.

Richard Wistar, Sr., a Quaker, reported that he has been providing soup to the occupants of the Old Stone Jail at Third and Market Streets for 11 years. Prior to that, the prisoners were starving. He formed the Philadelphia Society for Assisting Distressed Prisoners but his group was disbanded during the British occupation of 1777. A motion was made to elect Wistar president of Philadelphia Society for Alleviating the Miseries of Public Prisons. It passed by unanimous vote.

It was reported that disgraceful conditions exist in the Walnut Street jail built in 1773. Many prisoners are naked, having traded their clothing for food from the jailers. This has led to two deaths and four cases of frostbite in the past month.

It was unanimously agreed that prisoners deserve to be treated like fellow humans with all the same comforts, if not freedoms. The government must provide adequate food, clothing, and shelter for all detainees.

A motion was made for members William Barr, Richard Wistar, Ben Franklin, and John Richardson to investigate the existing conditions at all of the city's jails with the goal of recommending a reformative strategy.

The members are in agreement that the solution to the disorder and corruption in most prisons lies in solitary confinement at hard labor for each inmate for his or her entire sentence. This system has been tried and abandoned in England. It was due to cost and inadequate housing. Here in America, we shall perfect the method for the benefit of our fellow citizens.

Meeting adjourned at 8:05 p.m.

Respectfully submitted,

Elijah Watson

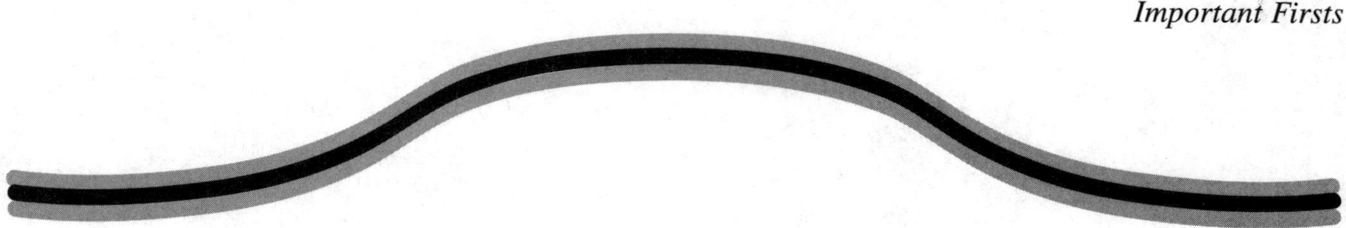

Prison Reform at Eastern State Penitentiary

1. Which task didn't the Eastern State Penitentiary inmates learn how to do?
   a. make shoes
   b. make tools
   c. dye fabric
   d. cane chairs
2. The Philadelphia Society for Alleviating the Miseries of Public Prisons believed that criminals
   a. should never be released back into society.
   b. should be converted to Buddhism.
   c. could change for the better while in prison.
   d. would be driven insane by solitary confinement.
3. The Eastern State Penitentiary accommodations were considered luxurious because few people had
   a. flush toilets or central heat in their homes.
   b. a chance to learn a trade (occupation).
   c. rooms in their homes as large as an inmate's cell.
   d. natural lighting in their homes.
4. The system of having prisoners work and live in solitary confinement had already failed in another country before it was tried at Eastern State Penitentiary. True or False? Explain.

   ____

   ____

   ____

5. Describe two of the terrible conditions that inmates faced at the time of the first meeting of the Philadelphia Society for Alleviating the Miseries of Public Prisons.

   ____

   ____

   ____

   ____

   ____

6. Would the Pennsylvania System have worked if it had not included solitary confinement? Defend your stance.

   ____

   ____

   ____

   ____

   ____

Civil War Battleship Crews:
The First Integrated U.S. Armed Forces

Almost all Civil War warships were wooden, used sails, and moved at a top speed of 15 miles per hour. Before the maiden voyage, men hid coins under the main mast to ensure that the crew would go to heaven in the event of a shipwreck.

Women did not go to sea; in fact, they could only board a ship as guests while in a port. But these ships were progressive in another way: They had the first integrated male crews in the U.S. armed forces. African Americans made up 20 percent of the Navy during the Civil War. A male could volunteer at the age of 12 and would serve for at least three years. There were plenty of jobs to do. Water continually collected in the ship's bottom and had to be pumped out by hand. Ballast bars lay in the ship's base. Hundreds of these iron or lead bars were moved by hand to retrim (balance) the ship in rough seas. Men nicknamed "powder monkeys" operated the cannons. It took three people to load and fire each of the two dozen cannons. The roar of a cannon's blast below deck was deafening, and many men lost their hearing.

Life aboard a Civil War battleship wasn't easy. In the ship's galley, the cooks served oatmeal, dried cheese, dried fruits, and boiled salt pork. They also baked hardtack biscuits. Made of flour and water, they were so hard that they often chipped someone's tooth. Goats and chickens that lived onboard provided milk and eggs. The water for drinking and cooking was stored in iron tanks and tasted metallic. The men drank sauerkraut juice each day to prevent scurvy. The only time they got fresh fruits and vegetables was in a port.

Privacy was nonexistent. There were no toilets, so the sailors had to go to the front of the ship and hang over the edge to relieve themselves. Sometimes they fell overboard, and it wasn't easy to get back on the ship. The men slept below deck in hammocks strung from the ceiling. These hung a mere 18 inches from each other, so in heavy seas, they swung back and forth, hitting each other all night long. The captain and his officers fared better. The captain had his own cook and a private area to bathe and relieve himself. He and his officers ate the best food and slept in sturdy berths built into the ship's side.

Sickness was common. In the sick bay, men lay in hammocks that looked like canvas bassinets. The ship's doctor had to be an expert at amputation because that's how badly wounded limbs were handled. In less than 60 seconds most doctors could cut off a limb and stuff it with charpie. This cloth acted as a sponge to keep the person from bleeding to death. The patients battled yellow fever, typhus, malaria, and typhoid, but they rarely won.

By the end of the Civil War, the Union Navy was the most powerful naval force on Earth. It had more than 670 ships and 57,000 men. The integrated crews had done well, yet the U.S. military changed its official policy after the War. Soldiers and sailors were segregated by race, and nearly 85 years would pass before they served together again.

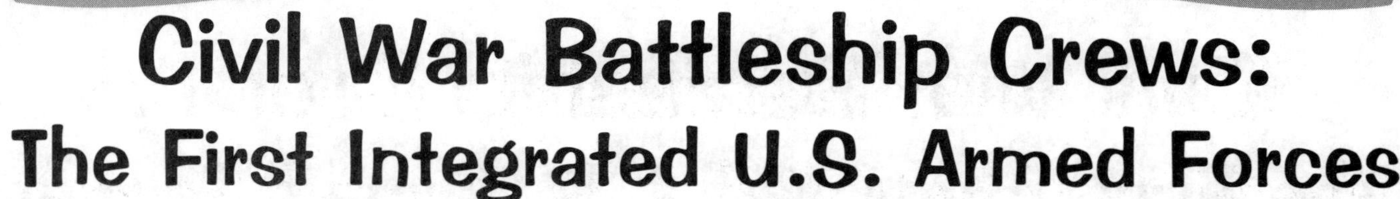

Civil War Battleship Crews:
The First Integrated U.S. Armed Forces

At the start of the Civil War Abraham Lincoln began a blockade of the Southern states. He hoped to shorten the war by preventing them from getting supplies. However, blockade runners often got past the Union ships in order to supply the South.

Captain Henry S. Stellwagen was the Civil War captain of the , the last all-sail ship built for the U.S. Navy. Serving beneath him was Yeoman* Moses Safford. These are notes from his log:

We are to cruise about the West Indies trying to capture Rebel privateers and cruisers and blockade runners.

The process of reasoning . . . seems to be that our ship is hought to be in European waters, and there is no United States warship resembling her cruising about here, and consequently she might approach closely to a Rebel vessel or blockade runner without exciting suspicion. - November 12, 1864 (off St. Thomas in the Caribbean)

We encountered a typical blockade runner—painted white and very sharply built . . . appeared to be waiting with fires banked for assurance from the shore that the coast was clear to run in. When, however, our ship headed in her direction, smoke began to come out of her funnel, and she made off to windward at good speed . . . we kept after her with all our sail and fired a gun for her to heave to. She did not accept the invitation nor heed the warning. She escaped into the fog. - December 19, 1864 (at sea)

*A yeoman is a U.S. Navy petty officer who performed clerical duties such as keeping records.

Safford, Moses. The USS Constellation. "Constellation History Civil War II."
http://www.constellation.org

Civil War Battleship Crews: The First Integrated U.S. Armed Forces

1. Sailors hid coins under the mast so that

a. they would win every battle.
b. their ship would not sink.
c. the crew would get along.
d. the crew would go to heaven if the ship went down.

2. In order to shoot cannonballs at enemy targets, powder monkeys used

a. gunpowder.
b. electricity.
c. a wood fire.
d. dynamite.

3. You can conclude that the blockade runner that the *USS Constellation* pursued was a

a. canoe
b. traditional ship with sails
c. steam ship
d. motorboat

4. Chickens and goats were kept aboard Civil War ships in order to provide fresh meat. True or False? Explain.

____

____

____

5. What reasons does Yeoman Safford give for why Captain Stellwagen believed that their ship could get close to blockade runners?

____

____

____

____

____

6. Was it fair that the ship's captain and officers had much better living conditions than the regular sailors? Defend your stance.

____

____

____

____

____

The Birth of Radio: The "Wireless"

Guglielmo Marconi was born in 1874 in Italy. He grew up to be the inventor who sent the first radio signals through the air. Even as a boy, sound waves interested him. By the time he was 21, he had sent radio signals through the air. Prior to that, sounds could only be sent through electrical wires in a telegraph system. Marconi used electromagnetic (radio) waves to send his signals. He called his system wireless telegraphy. He did hundreds of experiments. He found that having both the transmitter and receiver connected to earth and raising the antenna's height increased how far a signal could go. But the Italian government showed no interest in his invention! So he went to Great Britain to get a patent. A patent is a legal document. It states that an inventor has the sole right to make and sell an invention.

In 1899, Marconi sent a radio message across the English Channel to France. Just two years later he sent radio waves across the Atlantic Ocean. They went from Cornwall, England, to Newfoundland, Canada. That's a distance of more than 2,000 miles. Marconi sent his messages using Morse code, just as telegraph operators did.

Reginald Fessenden, an American, made the first wireless broadcast of speech and music in 1906. This set the stage for radio as we know it. Later that same year, he pioneered two-way wireless telegraphy. This gave ships a way to send distress signals. Ships used radio to bring rescuers to the shipwrecked in 1909 and in 1912. This saved thousands of lives and led to laws that require radios on passenger ships.

A ship's radio also led to the capture of Dr. Hawley Crippen. This man killed his wife. Then he buried her in his cellar. He and his mistress tried to escape from Great Britain. They got on the cruise ship posing as a father and teenage son. But they walked around holding hands. The captain got suspicious. He sent a wireless message to Scotland Yard. An inspector boarded the ship and arrested Crippen in Canada. He was the first killer caught via radio.

Now cell phones use radio waves. A cell phone connects to other phones via a radio tower. Each phone sends sounds over a unique frequency. But with so many Americans using cell phones, there aren't enough frequencies. Dividing regions into "cells" resolved this problem. Each cell has its own base station that does not let signals spread into other cells. Thus, the same frequencies can be used in cells that aren't near each other.

Marconi died in 1937. As a sign of respect, all wireless stations and transmitters worldwide shut down for one day.

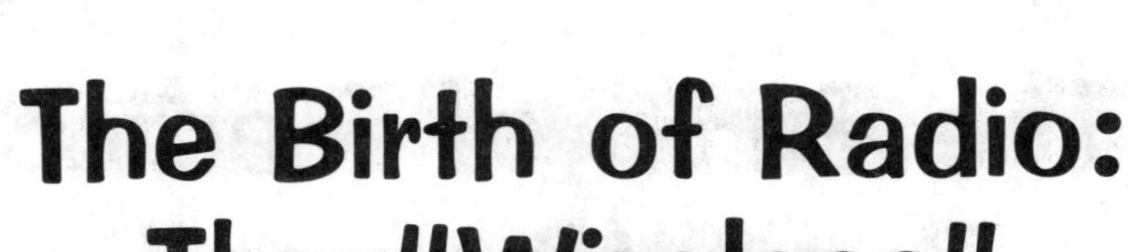

The Birth of Radio: The "Wireless"

THE MARCONI INTERNATIONAL MARINE COMMUNICATION COMPANY, Ltd.

"Have strong suspicions that Crippen London cellar murderer and accomplice are among saloon passengers. Accomplice dressed as a boy. Voice, manner, and build undoubtedly a girl."

Captain Henry Kendall

Wijesiri, Lionel. The Sunday Observer Online. "Famous trials that shook the world: The trial of Harvey Crippen"
http://www.sundayobserver.lk/2005/09/04/fea20.html

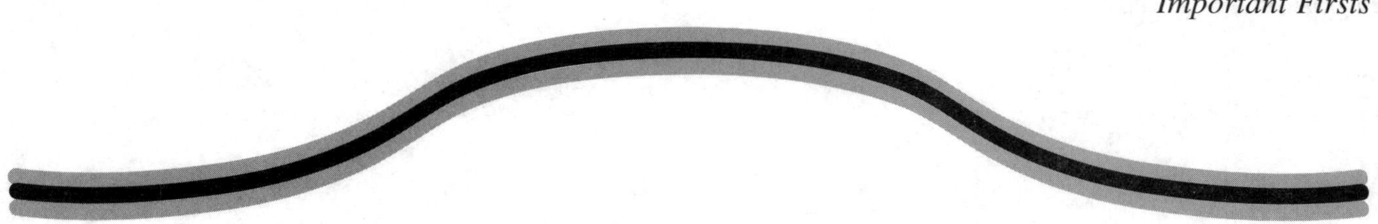

The Birth of Radio: The "Wireless"

1. Guglielmo Marconi received his wireless telegraphy patent from
   a. Italy.
   b. Great Britain.
   c. Canada.
   d. the United States of America.
2. The man who pioneered radio as we know it was
   a. Guglielmo Marconi.
   b. Henry Kendall.
   c. Hawley Crippen.
   d. Reginald Fessenden.
3. Dividing different areas into separate cells lets cell phones
   a. take photographs.
   b. access the Internet.
   c. send telegrams.
   d. use the same radio frequency in cells that are far apart.
4. The radio message sent at sea made Crippen's capture more certain than if Captain Kendall had waited until the ship had reached its destination and then contacted the police. True or False? Explain.

   ____

   ____

   ____

5. An accomplice is a partner in crime. Why did the wireless message the captain sent about Crippen call the criminal's companion an accomplice?

   ____

   ____

   ____

   ____

   ____

6. Should the U.S. government regulate the language and music that can be broadcast via radio? Defend your stance.

   ____

   ____

   ____

   ____

   ____

Henry Ford's Assembly Line

Henry Ford changed the world. Not by making the first car. He didn't do that, although he did make the first car that average people could afford. He helped more drivers get behind the wheel than any other person in history. But even more important, Ford invented a production method that changed how work was done in factories worldwide. His revolutionary ideas brought many manufactured goods within the reach of the masses.

From the time he was a teen, Ford was fascinated by the horseless carriages he had read about. He was a mechanical genius, and in 1891 he decided to build his own gas engine. He accomplished that goal in two years. Three years later he built a car that used the engine.

Ford and two partners started Ford Motor Company and began manufacturing cars in 1903. Each vehicle was assembled by one worker and cost $1,000. At that time only the wealthy could have one. Every one was painted black because that color paint dried fastest. In 1908 Ford began selling the Model T for $850. That price was still too high for most people. However, he sold over 10,000 in the first year. The company could not keep up with the demand. Ford wondered how he could speed up the production of a car. It took each Ford worker about 12.5 hours to build a single car.

Then Ford had a brilliant idea. He invented the assembly line. With it workers did one specific task, then passed the item on to another worker who would do something else. Gradually a larger item, such as an engine, was built. Inside the Ford factory, men stood beside a conveyor belt. This continuous moving belt transported the items from one place to another. As each engine moved past, one worker placed a bolt and nut. A person standing opposite him did the same on that side of the engine. Then the engine passed to other workers who tightened these nuts. Within one year this system cut the time it took to create one car to 90 minutes! Ford passed on to his customers the cost savings from using the assembly line.

Most of his employees hated the assembly line. They found it boring. In fact, half of all workers quit each year! Yet Ford knew that the only practical way to make affordable cars was with the assembly line. So in 1914 he decided to give his workers an incentive to stay. He reduced their workday by one hour and doubled their pay! Since most businesses made their workers toil long hours for low pay, people rushed to work in his factories.

The assembly line didn't just revolutionize the car industry. Factories everywhere picked up the system. The era of mass production had begun.

Henry Ford's Assembly Line

Model T Sales Flyer

Front of Sales Flyer

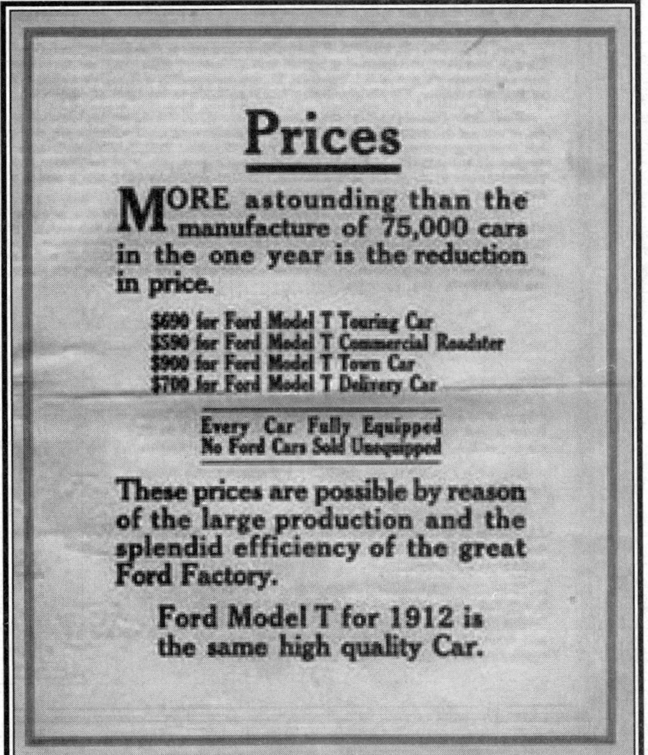

Prices

MORE astounding than the manufacture of 75,000 cars in the one year is the reduction in price.

$690 for Ford Model T Touring Car
$590 for Ford Model T Commercial Roadster
$900 for Ford Model T Town Car
$700 for Ford Model T Delivery Car

Every Car Fully Equipped
No Ford Cars Sold Unequipped

These prices are possible by reason of the large production and the splendid efficiency of the great Ford Factory.

Ford Model T for 1912 is the same high quality Car.

Back of Sales Flyer

One-third of all Cars made in America in 1912 will be Fords. What a Valuable Message to the World. That old, reliable 4-cylinder, 5-passenger Model T touring car, unchanged during its four years before the public. Is it any wonder that "When Ford speaks, the World listens"? If this were the announcement of a new model you might be skeptical of the car's merits, but Ford Model T is the best-known car on Earth.

Henry Ford Museum. "Model T Sales Literature."
http://www.hfmgv.org/exhibits/showroom/1908/fold.jpg

Henry Ford's Assembly Line

1. The first year Ford Motor Company produced cars,
   a. each one cost $850.
   b. Henry Ford invented the assembly line.
   c. almost everyone could afford to buy a car.
   d. it took one worker more than 12 hours to make one car.
2. Henry Ford built his first gas-powered engine in
   a. 1891.
   b. 1893.
   c. 1903.
   d. 1908.
3. The invention of Ford's assembly line was even more important than his creation of affordable cars because it
   a. made custom-made vehicles easier to produce.
   b. made Henry Ford rich.
   c. changed the way that factories operated around the world.
   d. created more jobs.
4. By 1912, a person could buy a Ford Model T Touring Car for $900. True or False? Explain.

   ____

   ____

   ____

5. Describe three important points in the 1912 sales flyer meant to encourage the reader to buy a Ford car. Use specifics from the sales flyer.

   ____

   ____

   ____

   ____

   ____

6. Was it wise for Ford Motor Company to pass along the savings gained by the assembly line to its customers by lowering car prices? Defend your stance.

   ____

   ____

   ____

   ____

   ____

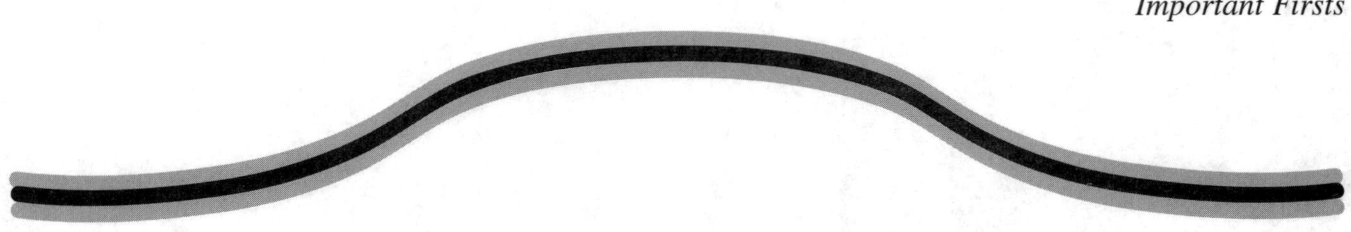

Charles Lindbergh and the First Transatlantic Flight

After World War I there was a surplus of airplanes and trained pilots. This led to the growth of airlines. But at first the planes just carried mail. Believe it or not, airmail pilots had a dangerous job. In fact, their survival rate was only about 900 flight hours! Still, people were delighted with flight.

In 1919, a wealthy man offered $25,000 to anyone who could fly nonstop from New York to Paris. Such a transatlantic flight was hazardous. The pilot would have to fly thousands of miles over a stormy sea and face thunderclouds, dense fog, and even icebergs. (Planes didn't fly as high then as they do now.) Over the next eight years several pilots tried to complete the journey, but each one failed. Then in May 1927 an unknown airmail pilot named Charles Lindbergh accepted the challenge.

His plane, the *Spirit of St. Louis*, was ill-equipped for such a dangerous trip. It had no radio. In order to carry all the fuel necessary, there was no room for excess weight. All that Lindbergh had with him was a quart of water, a paper bag of sandwiches, a map, and a rubber raft. Yet staying alert throughout the 33 1/2-hour flight proved to be the biggest problem for Lindbergh.

A cheering crowd greeted Lindbergh when he landed in Paris. After meeting European kings and princes, the pilot flew his plane home. There he was met with parades and parties. He was a world hero at the age of 25. Lindbergh's achievement inspired a popular song, a dance, and even fashions. Congress gave him the Medal of Honor made of gold. It is awarded to those who show courage, risk of life, and actions above and beyond the call of duty.

Lindbergh came to regret his fame. He refused numerous offers for moneymaking opportunities following his historic flight. Then in March 1932, his small son was kidnapped for ransom. Although he paid the money they demanded, the toddler died in the kidnappers' care.

After his body was found, Lindbergh and his family went to Europe and stayed for several years. They returned to America just before the nation entered World War II. Then Lindbergh flew 50 combat missions.

Charles Lindbergh and the First Transatlantic Flight

WANTED

INFORMATION AS TO THE
WHEREABOUTS OF

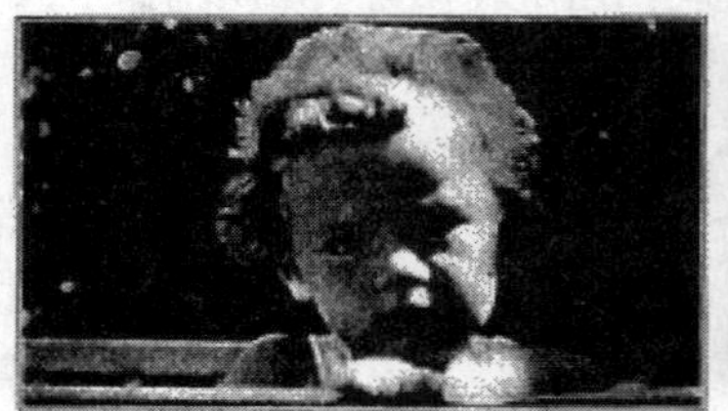

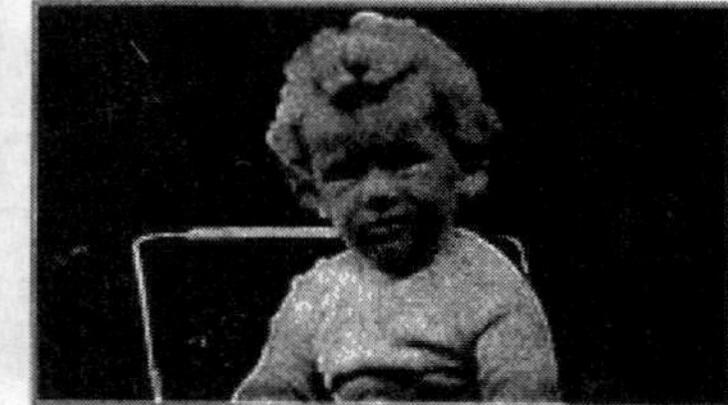

CHAS. A. LINDBERGH, JR.

OF HOPEWELL, N. J.

SON OF COL. CHAS. A. LINDBERGH

World-Famous Aviator

This child was kidnaped from his home in Hopewell, N. J., between 8 and 10 p. m. on Tuesday, March 1, 1932.

DESCRIPTION:

Age, 20 months
Weight, 27 to 30 lbs.
Height, 29 inches
Hair, blond, curly
Eyes, dark blue
Complexion, light
Deep dimple in center of chin
Dressed in one-piece coverall night suit

ADDRESS ALL COMMUNICATIONS TO
COL. H. N. SCHWARZKOPF, TRENTON, N. J., or
COL. CHAS. A. LINDBERGH, HOPEWELL, N. J.

ALL COMMUNICATIONS WILL BE TREATED IN CONFIDENCE

March 11, 1932

COL. H. NORMAN SCHWARZKOPF
Supt. New Jersey State Police, Trenton, N. J.

Charles Lindbergh and the First Transatlantic Flight

1. What didn't Lindbergh have aboard his plane during his historic flight?
   a. food
   b. a raft
   c. water
   d. a radio
2. How many years passed between the reward being offered for the first transatlantic flight and someone collecting the money?
   a. 1 year
   b. 5 years
   c. 8 years
   d. 12 years
3. During World War II Lindbergh flew combat missions for which nation?
   a. the United States
   b. Great Britain
   c. Germany
   d. Japan
4. In 1932, Charles Lindbergh lived in New Jersey. True or False? Explain.

   ____

5. Why did the kidnappers think that Charles Lindbergh had the money to pay for ransom?

   ____

6. Was Charles Lindbergh wrong to pay the ransom money to the kidnappers? Defend your stance.

   ____

A Giant Leap for Mankind

When President John F. Kennedy was sworn into office in 1961, he vowed to put a man on the moon by 1970. He did not live long enough to see his dream come true, but it did happen eight years later.

It was the morning of July 16, 1969. Three astronauts squeezed through the hatch of the spacecraft that would be their home for the next eight days. This was the crew of the mission. They intended to be the first men to step on the moon.

Neil Armstrong, Buzz Aldrin, and Michael Collins listened to a voice at launch control as it counted down the last ten seconds before liftoff. Clouds of steam and smoke billowed around the rocket as all the engines ignited. Slowly it lifted from the ground. Its destination was nearly 250,000 miles away.

Several rockets were used to boost the spacecraft into space. Two and a half minutes into the flight, the first stage had shut down. It fell into the Atlantic Ocean. Four seconds later, the second stage separated. The astronauts began to feel weightless. After the third and final stage fired, the spacecraft orbited Earth one and a half times before being propelled toward the moon.

On the fifth morning, NASA Mission Control woke up the astronauts. It was July 20—moon landing day! The spacecraft would split into two parts. Collins stayed in the . Aldrin and Armstrong got into the . Collins released the switch, and the two modules drifted apart. Less than two hours later, began its landing as the two men skillfully piloted the craft toward the moon's rocky surface. Meanwhile Collins kept orbiting the moon.

Neil Armstrong was the first man down the ladder. A camera mounted on the side of the let millions watch on television as he stepped onto the moon's surface and said, "That's one small step for a man, one giant leap for mankind." For two and a half hours the astronauts collected rocks and took photographs. Both men jumped high to enjoy the moon's gravity, which is weaker than Earth's. They set up a seismograph to detect lunar quakes and a laser reflector to bounce back beams from Earth. This would let scientists calculate the precise distance to the moon.

Before the men left, they put a plaque on the moon. It read, "We came in peace for all mankind." Nearby they planted the American flag. Since the moon has no wind, this flag had a special wire sewn along the top and bottom edges to make it look as if it were flying.

A Giant Leap for Mankind

July 22, 1969
Times Union
55 Exchange Boulevard
Rochester, NY 14614

Dear Editor:

The TV stations never tire of running newsreels of the astronauts. Everyone is all excited about our landing men on the moon a few days ago. Well, I am not one of them. I think that NASA has spent a ridiculous sum of money to accomplish this when there are many more pressing matters to which the funds could be applied here on Earth.

Think about the number of children born into poverty in the United States alone. The $1.9 billion that NASA spent achieving this goal could've been invested in those children. Then the money would have given us dividends called productive citizens. Just what are the dividends of the space program? How is my life—or yours for that matter—any better because men stood on the moon, gathered up rocks, and left an American flag?

Now there's already talk of another moon mission—for what purpose? What about the millions of people starving in Third World nations? Apparently we should just tell them, "Sorry you have to die, but we're going to spend our money on more important things like going to the moon. We're excited about showing off to the world our technological prowess." I'm sure that this explanation should satisfy all those people who are starving to death.

I challenge your readers to tell me what we have gained for our vast expenditure. I think NASA and the citizens of the United States should remember that "pride goeth before the fall."

Sincerely,

Winifred B. Hannamaker

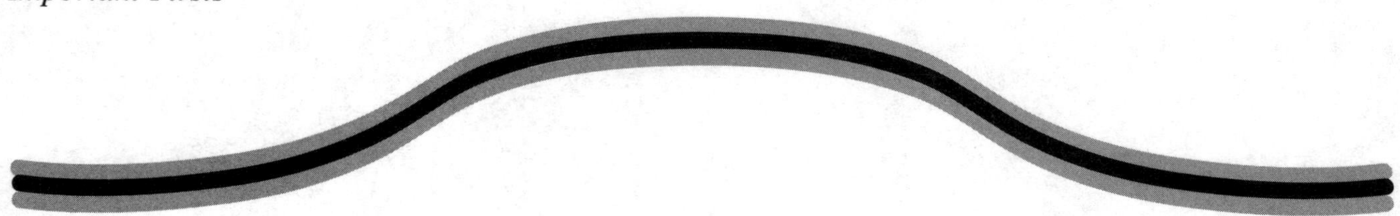

A Giant Leap for Mankind

1. Which man was the first to step onto the moon?
   a. Neil Armstrong
   b. John F. Kennedy
   c. Buzz Aldrin
   d. Michael Collins

2. What did the astronauts leave on the moon?
   a. a plaque
   b. an American flag
   c. a plaque and an American flag
   d. a plaque, an American flag, and scientific equipment

3. The moon rocks collected allowed scientists to determine the
   a. elements on the moon.
   b. age of the moon.
   c. distance to the moon.
   d. the age of and elements on the moon.

4. The moon's gravity is about the same as Earth's gravity. True or false? Explain.

   ____

   ____

   ____

5. What are the letter writer's two main criticisms of the *Apollo 11* mission?

   ____

   ____

   ____

   ____

   ____

6. Do you agree with the letter writer? Defend your stance.

   ____

   ____

   ____

   ____

   ____

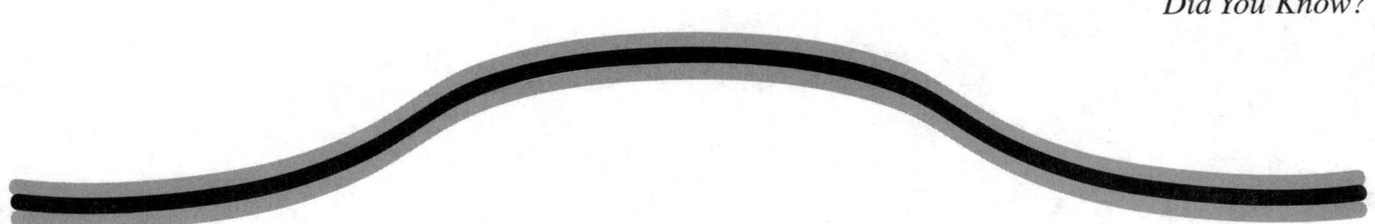

Executed for Espionage

Did you know that in 1953 two Americans were executed for espionage (spying)? It caused an uproar at the time. The U.S. Supreme Court and the American public were divided over whether or not they had been treated fairly.

The Cold War started at the end of World War II. The two world powers, the United States and Russia, did not fight openly. But each nation felt the other followed the wrong policy. The United States had capitalism and democracy. Russia had Communism and strict government controls. Russia wanted Communism to spread. The United States was determined not to let it.

It was a tough time for Americans who liked Communism. Many U.S. citizens thought to be spies for the Russians went to trial. Two of these were Ethel and Julius Rosenberg. They went to Communist meetings and read a Communist newspaper. In 1950 they were accused of espionage. The arrest record stated that Julius had given top-secret documents to a Russian spy. These papers helped Russia to build its first atomic bomb. The U.S. government had a decent case against Julius, but it had no proof against Ethel. The police actually arrested her to make her husband confess. It didn't work.

In court Ethel and Julius acted angry, and this made the jury dislike them. The only evidence against Ethel was her brother's and sister-in-law's statements. Her brother, David Greenglass, said that he had given Julius a diagram that showed a lens used in making the bomb. He said that Ethel had typed some papers. Both the Rosenbergs were found guilty of conspiracy and sentenced to death for treason. Yet neither one had been tried for that crime! This made their death sentences illegal.

The couple appealed their case. It went all the way to the U.S. Supreme Court. Four judges voted to stop their executions. But five votes were needed. In their jail, a phone had a direct line to the FBI. They were told that if they confessed, they would live. Although they had two young sons who would become orphans, the Rosenbergs refused to confess. They declared their innocence until they died on June 19, 1953. They were the only people put to death for spying during the 40 years of the Cold War.

In 1995, the U.S. government released 49 telegrams that had been found during the 1940s. The telegrams show that Julius worked as an agent for Russia. The Rosenbergs' sons say that they are fake.

America's spy agency is the CIA. Russia's is the KGB. In 1997, former KGB agent Alexsandr Feklisov stated that Julius helped him. The sketch Julius gave him was useful, but it had not played a big role in helping the Russians build an atomic bomb. He also said Ethel was not a spy. She may have known what her husband was doing, but she had never met with Feklisov.

Executed for Espionage

Many people demonstrated in New York and Washington to protest the Rosenbergs' death sentence. This poster urges people to take action:

ROSENBERGS' WEDDING ANNIVERSARY

SET AS THEIR EXECUTION DATE

TWO YOUNG SONS WILL BECOME ORPHANS

THIS IS AMERICAN JUSTICE?

The Rosenbergs face the electric chair just days from now. Yet they continue to declare their innocence, even though they have been told, "Confess and you will live." Now we know why. They were convicted by the testimony of liars!

***An affidavit* from a Macy's department store employee** proves that David Greenglass lied when he said that the Russians gave the Rosenbergs the gift of an expensive table. The affidavit states that the Rosenbergs bought the table, just as they had testified.

***Prosecution witness Max Elitcher** faces charges for making false statements to government officials while under oath. He admits that he hoped that testifying against the Rosenbergs would reduce his own sentence.

Veterans! You and your buddies fought and died for the freedoms and rights of all American citizens. Don't let this travesty of justice occur!

Show your support—join our protest in Union Square on Friday, June 12, 1953 at 4 P.M.

WRITE OR WIRE PRESIDENT EISENHOWER

DEMAND JUSTICE FOR THE ROSENBERGS!

CITIZENS TO SAVE THE ROSENBERGS

197 86TH STREET, NEW YORK, N.Y.

*An affidavit is a sworn statement.

Executed for Espionage

1. When the Rosenbergs' case went before the U.S. Supreme Court, how many justices voted to stop their executions?
   a. 2 justices
   b. 3 justices
   c. 4 justices
   d. 5 justices

2. David Greenglass gave testimony against
   a. his sister and brother-in-law.
   b. his wife.
   c. Alexsandr Feklisov.
   d. his brother and sister-in-law.

3. Why does the poster urge people to contact President Eisenhower?
   a. He was unaware that the Rosenbergs were going to be executed.
   b. He did not know that the Rosenbergs' sons would become orphans if their parents were executed.
   c. There was new evidence that the president had not been told about.
   d. Only he had the power to stop the Rosenbergs' execution.

4. Both of the Rosenbergs were convicted of treason. True or False? Explain.

____

____

____

5. State two of the poster's statements that appeal to the reader's emotions. Why were emotional statements used?

____

____

____

____

____

6. Should either or both of the Rosenbergs have been executed? Defend your stance.

____

____

____

____

____

Mascots in the Military

Did you know that animals have served as U.S. military mascots? The first records of them appear during the Civil War. The pets helped to keep spirits high during dangerous times. Caring for these animals reminded soldiers and sailors of their beloved pets back home. Petting their fur helped to ease stress, and the pets relieved boredom while the men awaited orders. Mascots were so important to morale that if enemy troops learned that there was one, they deliberately tried to kill it in order to break the men's spirit.

The men grew very fond of these animals. During the Civil War, Sallie, a Staffordshire Bull Terrier, was the mascot of the 11th Pennsylvania Volunteer Infantry. The men found her as a tiny puppy on a battlefield, and she followed them everywhere until a bullet struck her during the battle of Gravelly Run in Virginia. When the regiment's veterans erected a monument in 1890, they insisted on including their mascot. She had stood by their sides on the most frightening days of their lives.

Another Civil War regiment had a tame eagle. Traveling with an Ohio regiment was a cat, a dog, and a tame raccoon. General Robert E. Lee had a pet hen with him during the entire war.

Stubby served 18 months during World War I. This pit bull is the most decorated military dog in U.S. history. He smelled the poison gas used by the Germans before the men did and let them know when to put on their gas masks. He caught a German spy by the seat of his pants, and he saved the life of a little girl in Paris. He grabbed her dress and yanked her out of the way of a speeding car.

Ship mascots started living aboard U.S. Coast Guard cutters around 1900. At one point a black bear was the mascot on the cutter ! At other times an eagle and a goat served. Sinbad, a mutt, served the longest. He lived aboard the Coast Guard cutter for 11 years. Pete was another mutt who served during World War II. As the ship came in to dock, he would leap into the water and grab the rope. Then he would jump onto the dock and bring the rope to the mooring post. His antics made everyone smile.

During World War II, U.S. Navy ship crews also kept mascots. Dogs were the most common choice, followed by cats. Camouflage was a Navy cat. He fearlessly chased bullets when they sped across the ship's deck!

Mascots in the Military

This monument stands on Oak Ridge in Gettysburg, Pennsylvania. The full-size bronze Union soldier looks over the fields where the Confederate troops made their fatal charge. What makes this monument so unique is the bronze figure of a small dog lying at its base.

Here are the words on the plaque above the dog:

Total Enrollment 2096				
Killed & died of wounds	12 officers	219 men	total	231
Wounded	43 officers	729 men	total	772
Died of disease, etc.	4 officers	167 men	total	171
Captured or missing	5 officers	253 men	total	258
Total casualties				1432

Cedar Mountain, Rappahannock Station, Thoroughfare Gap, Bull Run

(2d), Chantilly, South Mountain, Antietam, Fredericksburg, Chancellorsville,

Gettysburg, Mine Run, Wilderness, Spotsylvania, North Anna, Totopotomoy,

Bethesda Church, Cold Harbor, Petersburg, Weldon Railroad, Dabney's Mill,

Boydton Plank Road (Gravelly Run), Five Forks, Appomattox

Courtesy of Randy Chadwick **http://www.brotherswar.com**

Mascots in the Military

1. The purpose of a military mascot is to
   a. protect the troops from the enemy.
   b. catch enemy spies.
   c. keep up the troops' spirits.
   d. give the troops experience in owning a pet.

2. Which mascot served the longest in the U.S. Coast Guard?
   a. Stubby
   b. a bear
   c. Sallie
   d. Sinbad

3. You can conclude that Stubby
   a. was trained to keep children out of traffic.
   b. sometimes wore a gas mask (put on him by the men).
   c. chased raccoons.
   d. stood guard over dead bodies on the battlefield.

4. The 11th Pennsylvania Volunteer Infantry fought two battles after their mascot died. True or False? Explain.

____

____

____

5. Was a casualty of the 11th Pennsylvania Volunteer Infantry most likely to be dead, wounded, or missing? Use information from the plaque in your answer.

____

____

____

____

____

6. During the war in Iraq, U.S. ground forces were not allowed to have animal mascots. They were under orders to shoot stray animals that terrorists could have infected with disease or packed with explosives and sent into camp. Was this policy wise? Defend your stance.

____

____

____

____

____

Destroying Ecosystems

Did you know that people cause big problems in an ecosystem when they get rid of species? In Malawi, Africa, people were upset. Leopards killed their cattle and dogs. The government agreed to let farmers kill every leopard they saw. After they did so, baboons had no predators. Their population grew rapidly. Then the baboons ate the people's crops. They caused worse problems than the leopards had.

In the early 1980s the farmers in Indonesia used insecticides. They wanted to kill the brown plant hoppers that ate the rice crop. But these chemicals also killed the spiders and bees that ate the plant hoppers. (By eating the insects, the toxin built up within their bodies.) To make matters even worse, the plant hoppers developed resistance to the chemicals. Without natural predators, they grew out of control. In 1986 the Indonesian government banned insecticides. Instead it brought in bees and spiders. At last the number of plant hoppers fell. Immediately the rice harvest increased by 4.5 million tons a year.

People can damage the environment by bringing in foreign species, too. More than 30 years ago, Asian carp were imported to farms in Arkansas. They were supposed to clean algae from ponds. Flooding swept them into the Illinois River. These fish are not very tasty. And now they are destroying the food source of fish that are edible. People don't want them to spread into the Great Lakes. So there are now underwater electrical gates to keep them from entering Lake Michigan.

Even pets can cause trouble in the environment. When a pair of pet skunks escaped on an island, they wreaked havoc with its ecosystem. They ate mice, moles, and birds' eggs. The skunks also had lots of babies. Meanwhile the number of birds, mice, and moles went down. The number of owls fell, too.

People cause trouble when they ruin environments as well. This has happened with wetlands. People fill in these damp, low-lying areas to build farms, homes, and malls. But mosquitoes breed out of control when wetlands are drained. At first scientists couldn't figure out why this happened. Then they realized that rain water puddles offered mosquitoes places to breed without providing homes for the predators that eat them. A single duckling eats at least 2,000 mosquito larvae a day, but ducks can't live in puddles. To test their theory, scientists restored a 1,500-acre wetland. In a short time the mosquito population fell by 90 percent!

Destroying Ecosystems

Today's Environment **December 17, 2008**

Trouble in a Striped Shell

A small animal invaded the Great Lakes more than 20 years ago. Very tiny and sporting a striped shell, no one realized the significance of the first appearance in 1986. But these zebra mussels were about to change the underwater environment of the Great Lakes in a major way.

Ships cross the Atlantic Ocean, head down the St. Lawrence Seaway, and enter the Great Lakes. At least one vessel coming from the sea brought the mussels as stowaways on its hull. The zebra mussels were native to salt water and should've died in the fresh water of the Lakes . . . but they didn't. Instead they adapted and started to take over. They had no natural predators, so they reproduced at an explosive rate. They soon spread throughout all five of the Great Lakes.

Zebra mussels eat algae, which leads to clearer water. Sounds like a good thing, right? That was people's first reaction. They liked the improvement in water quality. But not for long. The water soon became so clear that sunlight could penetrate deeper than ever before. For the first time in recorded history, fish in the Great Lakes started getting skin cancer.

Removing the algae made the water more acidic, too. And to top it all off, there's so many zebra mussels that they've eaten the algae that native species needed for survival. Native fish have been dying in droves. Some species have even disappeared from the Lakes.

More than two decades later, we're still stumped by these tiny invaders. The only thing we know for sure is that they're extremely hard to eliminate. The best way to keep them from spreading is to destroy them. A recent law ensures that whenever a vessel—even a pleasure boat—is placed in dry dock, its hull must be scraped to eliminate these pests. Will it work? Only time will tell.

Destroying Ecosystems

1. A natural predator for mosquitoes is a

a. duck.
b. baboon.
c. brown plant hopper.
d. skunk.

2. Once the brown plant hoppers were resistant to the insecticide, the chemical

a. made the bugs grow bigger than ever before.
b. started to kill the bugs.
c. no longer killed the bugs.
d. made the bugs unable to reproduce.

3. What do you think they did in Africa to control the baboon population?

a. They used insecticides.
b. They restored wetlands.
c. They built underwater electrical gates.
d. They reintroduced a few leopards.

4. Just like the zebra mussel, the Asian carp was introduced into the Great Lakes accidentally. True or False? Explain.

____

____

____

5. Describe the three major problems the zebra mussels are causing for the Great Lakes.

____

____

____

____

____

6. Should there be stiff monetary penalties for people who knowingly bring an exotic animal into an environment or release a pet into the environment? Defend your stance.

____

____

____

____

____

The U.S. Coast Guard

Did you know that the U.S. Coast Guard is the fifth branch of the armed services? Its main goal is to insure national security. This means protecting people, the environment, and shipping interests. To do this, the Coast Guard must patrol more than 95,000 miles of coastline. This includes ports, harbors, and inland water routes in the United States, Puerto Rico, and a few Pacific islands.

The U.S. Department of Homeland Security runs the Coast Guard. But the U.S. Navy takes command during a war. The U.S. Coast Guard motto is "Semper paratus." This Latin phrase means "Always ready." New recruits learn the skills needed in the Coast Guard at boot camp, which lasts eight weeks. Recruits must learn how to use weapons and do first aid. The men and women learn how to survive in the water and operate ship radios, too. New members may also go to the Coast Guard Academy. At the end of four years, the cadets earn an officer's rank as well as a college degree. Then they serve as junior officers aboard Coast Guard cutters.

The main vessel used by the U.S. Coast Guard is a cutter. In 1831 a cutter rescued people at sea for the first time. Now search and rescue is one of the Coast Guard's major duties. Vessels in distress may be cargo ships in the ocean or pleasure craft on a lake. The Coast Guard tries to prevent accidents, too. So each year it does safety inspections on 34,000 American boats, ships, and barges. It inspects 19,000 foreign vessels for safety as well.

The Coast Guard runs the International Ice Patrol. An iceberg hit the *Titanic* in 1912 and caused more than 1,500 people to die. In 1913, a group of 17 nations agreed to have an ice patrol. They wanted to keep such a tragedy from happening again. Each day the Ice Patrol watches for icebergs in the shipping lanes of the North Atlantic Ocean. Aircraft and icebreakers patrol a huge area. They warn ships about the icebergs or they try to destroy them. Icebreakers are Coast Guard cutters designed to crush and break ice. These ships also bring supplies to the researchers living in Antarctica.

How important is the Coast Guard? Look at the facts. Every day the U.S. Coast Guard conducts 82 search and rescue missions. This helps 114 people in distress and saves 15 lives. It also protects $4.9 billion in property and helps with the clean up of 11 oil or chemical spills. In addition, it seizes $2.4 million of illegal drugs and stops 26 illegal immigrants from reaching the U.S. shore.

The U.S. Coast Guard

This is a 1917 U.S. Coast Guard recruitment poster.

Courtesy of the Library of Congress, "Men Wanted for the U.S. Coast Guard," LC-USZC4-945

The U.S. Coast Guard

1. A person can earn a college degree by

a. serving as a junior officer for four years on a U.S. Coast Guard cutter.

b. taking classes at the U.S. Department of Homeland Security.

c. serving on a U.S. Coast Guard cutter for six years in any position.

d. attending the U.S. Coast Guard Academy.

2. Who takes charge of the U.S. Coast Guard during a war?

a. the U.S. Navy

b. the International Ice Patrol

c. the U.S. Department of Homeland Security

d. the U.S. Coast Guard Academy

3. Which is a service the U.S. Coast Guard does not perform?

a. clean up oil spills

b. regulate ship traffic in ports

c. search a boat for illegal drugs

d. stop illegal immigrants from entering the United States

4. The 1917 U.S. Coast Guard recruitment poster could be used today just as it is. True or False? Explain your answer.

____

____

____

5. Think about employment opportunities in the United States in 1917. Would the U.S. Coast Guard recruitment poster have attracted many applicants? Why or why not?

____

____

____

____

____

6. Would you consider joining the U.S. Coast Guard when you're an adult? Why or why not?

____

____

____

____

____

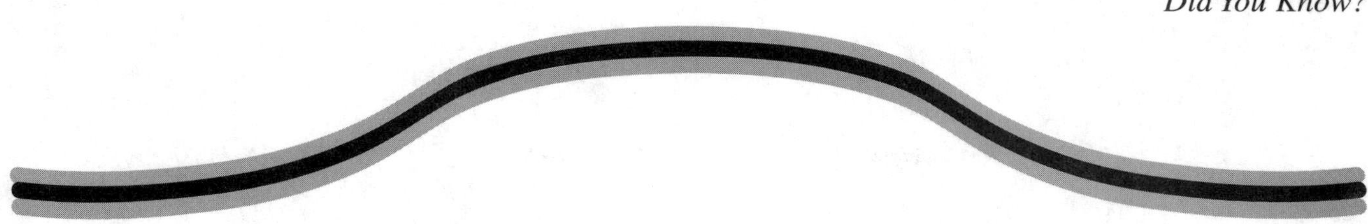

The Man Who Slept Through His Own Presidency

Would you believe that David Rice Atchison slept through the most important day of his life? It all happened on March 4, 1849. Government leaders were coming from all over the nation. They wanted to see Zachary Taylor sworn in as the 12th president of the United States. At that time March 4 was the inauguration date. (Today it is January 20.)

Courtesy of the Library of Congress, "David Rice Atchison," LC-USZ62-109952

The first three days of the month had had terrible, stormy weather. The roads, unpaved at that time, were muddy. They had deep ruts. Travel was slow. Few of the people who were expected to come had actually arrived. So it was decided that Taylor's inauguration would be postponed for 24 hours. That would give people more time to reach the capital.

Yet this meant that the prior president, James Polk, was no longer president. And neither was Taylor until he was sworn into office. So who would be the U.S. president during those 24 hours? According to the U.S. Constitution, the presidency passed to Senator David Rice Atchison. He was the president pro tempore of the U.S. Senate. The president pro tempore is elected by the Senate to preside when the vice president is not there. The Senate typically chooses the majority party senator with the longest continuous service for this honor. Sometimes the president pro tempore signs official papers for the Senate. But never before had one actually served as U.S. president!

Atchison never even knew that he was the president. The Missouri senator had been working overtime for several weeks. He was totally exhausted when he came in early on the morning of March 4. He told his housekeeper that he was going to lie down. Then he slept all that day and night. He awoke on March 5. He had slept through his presidency!

Atchison served as president pro tempore of the Senate from 1846 to 1854. But never again was he or any other president pro tempore the U.S. president.

The Man Who Slept Through His Own Presidency

DICTIONARY OF THE AMERICAN GOVERNMENT Congressional Law

Power of the purse. The power of the purse refers to the Constitutional right given to Congress to raise and spend money. This includes the power to levy taxes on constituents, spend revenue on specific causes, assume debt and liability, and pay off debt and liability including interest accrued.

President pro tempore. The Constitution provides for a president pro tempore. This senator is chosen by the rest of the senators to preside over the Senate when the vice president cannot be there. In the Presidential Succession Act of 1792, the president pro tempore was next in line of succession to the presidency after the vice president.

A law completely removed the president pro tempore from the line of succession in 1886. Cabinet members were used instead. In 1947 a new law changed the order of succession to its current status. It placed the Speaker of the House in line immediately after the vice president. The president pro tempore comes after the Speaker, and then the secretary of state and other cabinet officers follow in order of their departments' creation.

The president pro tempore holds the office until the election of another president pro tempore. However, the president pro tempore may chose another senator to preside in his or her temporary absence. Usually a member of the majority party is selected.

Previous questions. A motion to end debate and force an immediate vote on a pending measure. In some legislative bodies, this is called cloture.

The Man Who Slept Through His Own Presidency

1. The president pro tempore is elected by the
   a. U.S. president.
   b. voters of the United States.
   c. the U.S. vice president.
   d. the Senate.
2. David Rice Atchison
   a. was never the acting U.S. president.
   b. knew that he was the acting U.S. president.
   c. discovered that he had been the acting U.S. president after the fact.
   d. never knew that he had been the acting U.S. president.
3. The 11th president of the United States was
   a. Zachary Taylor.
   b. James Polk.
   c. David Rice Atchison.
   d. none of the above.
4. The president pro tempore has always been in the line of U.S. presidential succession. True or False? Explain.

   ____

   ____

   ____
5. Why is it essential to have a clear line of succession for the U.S. presidency?

   ____

   ____

   ____

   ____

   ____
6. Do you think that the current line of presidential succession is better or worse than prior ones? Defend your stance.

   ____

   ____

   ____

   ____

   ____

Scream Machines: The History of Roller Coasters

Did you know that roller coasters had their start nearly 600 years ago in Russia? The first one was primitive. In the 1400s Russians used their icy slopes to give thrill rides. The rider sat on a guide's lap as they slid down the slope on a sled with wheels. The first roller coaster with wheels on a track was built in Russia in 1804. Thrill seekers sat in single-person carts. They often fell out during the ride!

The first roller coaster that looked a little like a modern one was the Aerial Walk. It was built in France in 1817. Riders climbed to the top of a hill. Workers pushed the cars up the hill for the people to get in. They rode down a gentle curved slope, but even a leaf on the track could derail the car.

Roller coasters crossed the Atlantic when coal mine railways inspired the Mauch Chunk Switchback Railway. It opened in the Pennsylvania mountains in 1873. People rode an open train car down a long inclined slope. LaMarcus Adna Thompson, the father of the American roller coaster, rode it and had an idea. In 1884 he built the Switchback Railway at Coney Island near New York City. He charged a nickel a ride and earned hundreds of dollars a day.

The 1920s were the "Golden Age of Roller Coasters." Out-and-back wooden coasters were the most popular. They let riders soar up and down hills, around tight corners, and return to the station. Nearly 2,000 of them sprang up in America, including one of the world's most famous—the Cyclone at Coney Island. As new coasters were designed, some gave riders back or neck injuries. Such injuries were so common that before getting on some coasters, a person had to be examined in line by a nurse!

During the 1930s the Great Depression stopped roller coaster construction. Many parks shut down. During the 1940s the materials used to maintain the coasters went to the war effort. By the 1950s just half of the roller coasters erected in the 1920s still stood. But roller coasters were at the cusp of a new golden era much bigger than the first.

Walt Disney opened Disneyland in 1955. It was the first modern amusement park. Four years later he added the Matterhorn Bobsleds, the world's first steel roller coaster. Steel coasters allowed for more daring designs. They soon appeared in parks throughout the nation. By 1975, California had the Corkscrew, the world's first steel coaster that flipped riders upside down. In 1984 the King Cobra, the first stand-up roller coaster, was built in Ohio. Since then barrel rolls, tilting seats, and lying down coasters have thrilled riders.

Safety and comfort are top priorities. Roller coasters are tested many times before they have their first human rider. Today's tallest, fastest roller coaster is the Kingda Ka in New Jersey. Tomorrow it will be something else. Every new roller coaster is called the ultimate scream machine—combining terror with thrills. They are the most popular rides at any amusement park. People love the feeling they get from safely dropping 20 stories. How else could they get such amazing thrills . . . and live to do it again?

Scream Machines: The History of Roller Coasters

NEW!

The Komodo

The World's Fastest, Most Terrifying Roller Coaster!
Komodo dragons are one of the most fearsome predators on Earth. Dangerous and aggressive, they are relentless And so is the ride named in their honor. But don't take our word for it . . . find out for yourself!

FUN PASS

The holder of this pass is invited to a sneak preview of the Komodo, the World's Fastest, Most Terrifying Roller Coaster. You'll blast from 0 to 135 mph in 3 seconds, then rocket skyward 500 feet (50 stories) at a 90-degree angle! Glide through a heart-stopping twist as you plummet toward the ground at more than 110 mph. Fly over three camelbacks for major air time. Speed through the tightest death spiral ever built. As you race into the station, you'll be praying the brakes work.

Bring this pass with you on Sneak Preview Night, Friday, May 1. YOU MUST HAVE THIS PASS TO ENTER THE PARK. The park is not open for any other guests.

Be one of the first to ride the Komodo . . . if you dare!

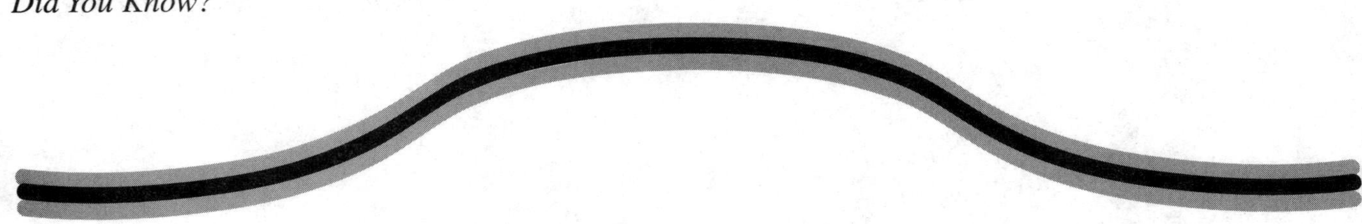

Scream Machines: The History of Roller Coasters

1. Coney Island's Cyclone is a

a. stand-up roller coaster.

b. America's first roller coaster.

c. wooden out-and-back roller coaster.

d. the world's first steel roller coaster.

2. The first modern amusement park was

a. not mentioned in the passage.

b. Disney World.

c. Coney Island.

d. Disneyland.

3. The very first "roller coasters" were most like

a. sledding hills.

b. railways built into mountainsides.

c. coal cars in coat mines.

d. carts pushed down a hill.

4. The invention of steel roller coasters brought about a new golden age for these scream machines. True or False? Explain.

____

____

____

5. Why did the designers give the Komodo roller coaster its name?

____

____

____

____

____

6. Would you like to ride the Komodo? Defend your stance.

____

____

____

____

____

Dorothea Dix, Champion for the Mentally Ill

Dorothea Dix was born in 1802. Her childhood was difficult. Her mother was mentally unstable, and her father drank too much. She had to raise her two little brothers without their help. When she grew up, she never wanted to marry.

She decided to spend her life teaching. This she did until she reached the age of 39. At that time she went to the East Cambridge Jail in Boston to teach Sunday school. She discovered men, women, and children together in unheated, filthy cells. Some were naked, hungry, and sleeping on stone floors. Others were chained to the wall. Many of these inmates suffered from mental illnesses. They had done nothing wrong. The situation so shocked Dix that she devoted the rest of her life working for reform.

Courtesy of the Library of Congress, "Dorothea Dix," LC-USZ62-9797

Dix believed that all people deserved to live in decent conditions. At the time, hers was a radical view. Some people said that mental illness was God's curse on a person's sins. Most people thought that the insane couldn't be cured. Living in awful conditions in a jail was all that they could expect. Yet Dix proved that not all mental illness is incurable. One example was a young woman called a "raging maniac." For years she had been chained inside a cage and whipped to control her speech. Dix asked a couple to take this woman into their home. Once she was treated like a human being, she slowly regained her sanity.

Dix went to jails and poorhouses, where most of the mentally ill lived, all over Massachusetts. She asked the state lawmakers to provide the funds for better conditions. Fortunately, she was a friend of the governor. This gave her influence with the legislature. Reforms began there and spread. New Jersey built the first state mental hospital as a result of her efforts.

By the time she was 54, Dix had covered half of the United States and some of Europe checking institutions for mistreatment. During the two-year period from 1854 to 1856 she made as many effective changes in the way Europeans dealt with the mentally ill as she had in the United States.

The Civil War interrupted her work for five years. During that time she served without pay as the head of the Union Army's nurses. As soon as the war ended, Dix went back to championing the rights of the mentally ill. She continued to work for this cause until she turned 80 and fell ill. Then she kept the problem before the public by writing numerous editorials. By the time she died, she had helped to start 32 mental hospitals, 15 schools for the feeble minded, a school for the blind, and nursing schools. Her efforts also led indirectly to many new and improved facilities for the mentally ill.

During her lifetime, people recognized that Dix was one of the greatest social reformers of the 19th century. Yet she was so modest that she refused to have any of the hospitals or schools named after her. Expressions of praise for her work made her blush. After her death, some institutions were renamed in her honor.

Dorothea Dix, Champion for the Mentally Ill

Dorothea Dix spent a great deal of time urging the government to offer funding or designate land for the building of mental hospitals. Here is the testimony that Dorothea Dix gave in front of the 31st Congress's first session on June 25, 1850:

"I pass by . . . nearly one hundred examples of insane men and women, in filthy cells, chained and hobbled . . . Some were confined in low, damp, dark cellars; some wasted their wretched existence in dreary dungeons, deserted and neglected. It would be fruitless to attempt describing the sufferings of these unhappy beings for a day even. What must be the accumulation of the pains and woes of years, consigned to prisons and poor-houses, to cells and dungeons, enduring every variety of privation -- helpless, deserted of kindred, tortured by fearful delusions, and suffering indescribable pains and abuses. These are no tales of fiction.

I believe that there is no imaginable form of severity, of cruelty, of neglect, of every sort of ill management for mind and body, to which I have not seen the insane subject in all our country. . . As a general rule, ignorance procures the largest measure of these shocking results. But, while of late years much is accomplished, and more is proposed, by far the largest part of those who suffer remain unrelieved, and most do so, except the General Government unites to assist the several States in this work."

This testimony appeared in the **Congressional Globe** 31st Congress, 1st Session, p. 1290.

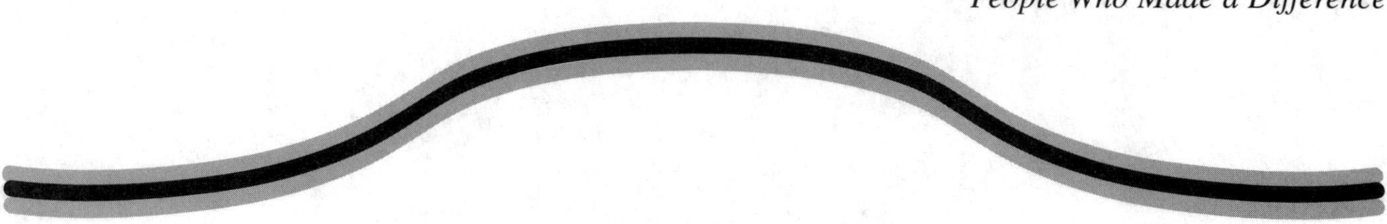

Dorothea Dix, Champion for the Mentally Ill

1. The first place where Dix successfully implemented reforms to help the mentally ill was

a. Europe.
b. Massachusetts.
c. New Jersey.
d. Washington, D.C.

2. Dix believed that the mentally ill

a. should have good living conditions.
b. should not be in institutions.
c. didn't realize that they were being mistreated.
d. were all curable given time and the right treatment.

3. Dix had to take a five-year break from her campaign for the mentally ill because she was

a. very ill.
b. taking care of her dying parents.
c. building schools for nurses and the blind.
d. directing the Union Army nurses.

4. In her testimony before Congress, Dix said that the mentally ill were mistreated. True or False? Use details from her testimony to support your answer.

____

____

____

5. What action does Dix urge in her testimony before Congress?

____

____

____

____

____

6. Do you think that today mental illness still carries more of a stigma (shame and embarrassment) than physical illness? Defend your stance.

____

____

____

____

____

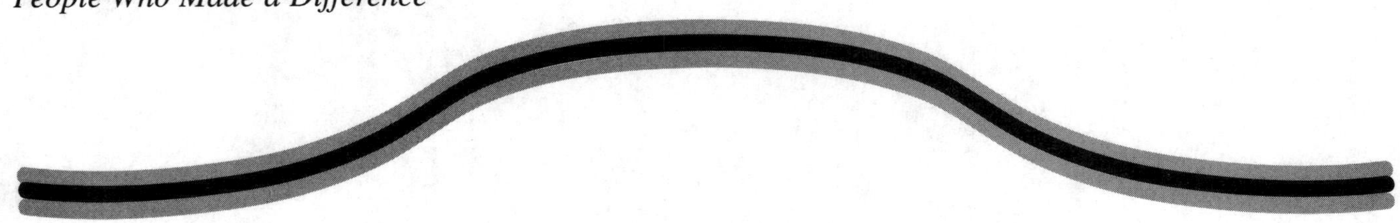

Thomas Edison, the Wizard of Menlo Park

Thomas Alva Edison is one of the greatest inventors in history. Yet his teacher told his mother that he was stupid! Mrs. Edison removed her son from the school and taught him herself. She found that not only did he love reading books, he could remember nearly everything he'd read. He built a chemical lab in his home. To get the money for supplies, he took a job carrying newspapers on a train. Then he set up a lab in a baggage car. But a chemical fire got both Edison and his equipment thrown off the train. Later a train accident damaged his hearing. He was almost deaf in his last years.

When he was 16, Edison found work as a telegraph operator. He started doing experiments with the telegraph equipment. He soon found ways to improve the device. His telegraph was faster. Instead of just one message, it sent four at once on a single wire. Alexander Graham Bell patented a crude telephone. Within a year Edison had made improvements that made the device practical. Edison wanted his inventions to be used. So he found financial partners to market his products. He used the income from early inventions to fund the creation of more. He was a millionaire by the time he was 45.

In 1876, he set up the first industrial research laboratory in the world at Menlo Park in New Jersey. He started to work on a way to record and play back messages sent via telegraph and telephone. This led to the phonograph, an ancient ancestor of a CD player. Using a metal disk, he was the first person to record and store sounds. As a result, Edison earned worldwide fame. People called him the Wizard of Menlo Park.

Next he made the electric light bulb. But since no one had electricity, what good was it? Edison set out to change that. In 1882 he set up the first electrical power plant. The Pearl Street Station in New York City used steam to make electricity. Wires carried the power from the plant to businesses and homes. By the 1890s, communities worldwide had copied his power plant. Thanks to his genius, the world had been transformed. It was a brighter place!

In 1892 Edison created General Electric Company. It made the lighting fixtures, outlets, lamps, and cords needed for electrical power. Next he turned his attention to creating a device to record and play back motion pictures. Later he designed the batteries used in cars and railroad signals.

Edison's most famous quote shows how much he valued hard work, "Genius is one percent inspiration and 99 percent perspiration." He had a goal: to invent something new every ten days! During one 4-year stretch, he got 300 U.S. patents. That's one for every five days! He patented 1,093 inventions. That's the most the U.S. Patent Office has ever issued to one person!

Edison died at the age of 84 on October 18, 1931. It was on the 52nd anniversary of his creation of the light bulb. On the evening of his funeral, U.S. President Herbert Hoover had the White House's lights dimmed for a short time. He asked people to do the same in their homes and businesses. The short darkness reminded them how Edison had brought light to many.

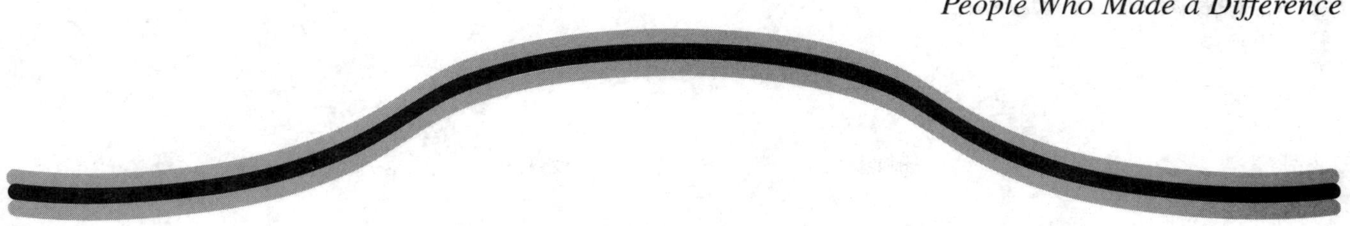

Thomas Edison, the Wizard of Menlo Park

Even great inventors sometimes come up with ideas that flop. Thomas Edison opened a cement plant in 1902. It lost money. So Edison decided to create his own demand with concrete houses. Today there are 12 surviving examples of his worst invention: the single-piece cast-concrete house.

Press Release

August 23, 1906

FOR IMMEDIATE RELEASE

NEW YORK CITY, NY: Thomas Edison has announced that concrete houses are the wave of the future. Poured in a single-mold monolith*, concrete houses will be fireproof, stormproof, insect-proof, and easy to clean. These dwellings, which can never rot, will be mass produced at Edison Portland Cement Works located in New Village, New Jersey. The first homes are expected to be erected in 1909.

Courtesy of the Library of Congress, "Thomas Edison's Concrete House," LC-USZ62-78947

Each house and all its fixtures, including sinks, shutters, and cabinets will be cast as a single monolith of concrete. The process takes just a few hours. Extra stories can be added to a dwelling with a simple adjustment of the molding forms. The walls will be pre-tinted in attractive colors and will never need repainting.

These homes will be the salvation of slum dwellers. Buyers will pay the amazing price of $1,200, one-third the cost of the average home today. This will put these homes within the reach of the poorest of the poor, and Edison emphasizes that he intends to make no profit from this venture. He feels compelled to do this so that the poor can have a better life than they currently do in the existing tenement slums.

*one large block

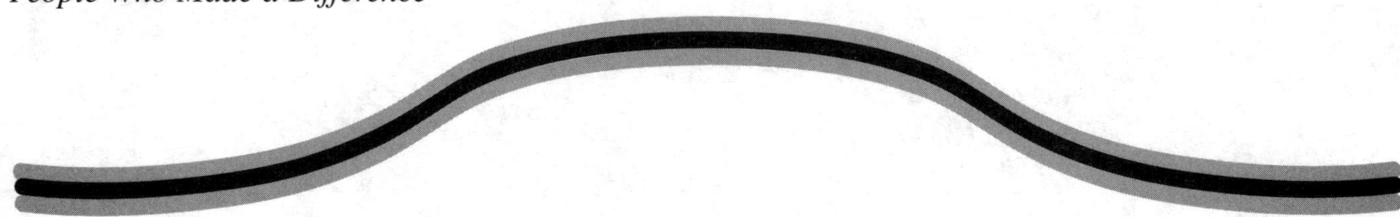

Thomas Edison, the Wizard of Menlo Park

1. What distinction is held by Thomas Edison?

a. first U.S. telegraph operator
b. the inventor of nuclear power plants
c. the holder of the most U.S. patents
d. first deaf person to create a video recording

2. The name of the world's first industrial research laboratory was

a. Wizard.
b. Menlo Park.
c. Pearl Street Station.
d. General Electric.

3. Which of the following items did Thomas Edison not invent?

a. electric light bulbs
b. phonographs
c. concrete houses
d. television

4. After Edison created concrete homes, he became a millionaire. True or False? Explain.

____

____

____

5. Why do you think that Edison's concrete houses never became popular? Give at least two reasons.

____

____

____

____

____

6. Do you think if concrete houses were reintroduced today that they would be successful? Defend your stance.

____

____

____

____

____

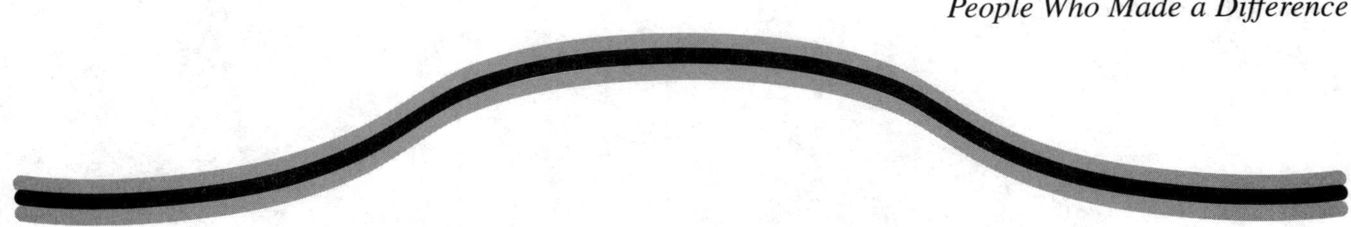

Mohandas Gandhi: A Man of Peaceful Action

The people of India call Mohandas Gandhi the father of their nation. They refer to him as Mahatma (Great Soul). He is one of the greatest leaders of the 20th century.

At first glance, no one would have considered Gandhi powerful. He was so thin his bones stuck out. But he was a towering man in terms of moral strength. He believed in treating all others with kindness. He felt that nonviolent solutions to problems could always be found. He said that how people behaved was far more important than what they achieved. He also said that it is honorable to go to jail for a just cause.

Gandhi was born in 1869 and got married at 13! Arranged marriages at that age were common then. He lived a simple life as a vegetarian. He didn't want to kill animals for food. He studied law and went to South Africa in 1893 to do legal work. There he met with discrimination. This was true for most Indians. He remained there for 22 years trying to end such prejudice. He developed a method of passive resistance and noncooperation to bring about social change. This method was based on the teachings of Jesus Christ and the written works of Leo Tolstoy and Henry David Thoreau. Years later Martin Luther King, Jr., adopted Gandhi's method to win civil rights for African Americans in the United States.

When Gandhi left South Africa, he went back to India. There he became the leader of the Indian nationalist movement. He taught his people to use nonviolent resistance to protest British rule. In his quest for Great Britain to grant India its independence, the British arrested him many times. He spent a total of seven years in prison. Yet he also worked for the British when he felt their cause was worthwhile.

The Amritsar Massacre took place in April 1919. A British general told his troops to shoot into an unarmed crowd. Nearly 400 Indians died. But Gandhi urged his followers not to react with more violence. Instead he fasted (went without food) to show that bloodshed was not the answer.

Finally, India gained its freedom in August 1947. But then the nation split in two as religious groups fought with one another. So Gandhi turned his peaceful protests to try to unite these groups. At last the religious leaders agreed to stop fighting. Just 12 days later, a man killed Gandhi! He opposed Gandhi's tolerance for all religions.

At Gandhi's funeral, Albert Einstein said, "Generations to come will scarcely believe that such a one as this walked the earth in flesh and blood."

Mohandas Gandhi: A Man of Peaceful Action

Great Britain was fighting for its very existence during the years 1939–1945. Germany was bombing the nation almost constantly. At the same time, Great Britian was in control of India.

Here is part of Mohandas Gandhi's Speech to the All-India Congress given in Bombay, India, on August 7, 1942:

> "I know full well that the Britishers will have to give us freedom when we have made sufficient sacrifices and proved our strength. We must remove any hatred for the British from our hearts. At least in my heart there is no such hatred. As a matter of fact, I am a greater friend of the British now than I ever was.
>
> The reason for this is that at this moment they are in distress. My friendship demands that I must make them aware of their mistakes. As I am not in the position in which they are, I can point out their mistakes. I know they are on the brink of a ditch and are about to fall into it. Therefore, even if they want to cut off my hands, my friendship demands that I should try to pull them out of that ditch.
>
> This is my claim, at which many people may laugh, but all the same I say this is true. At the time when I am not about to launch the biggest fight in my life there can be no hatred for the British in my heart. The thought that because they are in difficulties I should give them a push is totally absent from my mind. It never has been there. May be that in a moment of anger they might do things which might provoke you. Nevertheless you should not resort to violence and put non-violence to shame."

Vol. 76, April 1, 1942–December 17, 1942, pages 379–380. The Publications Division, Ministry of Information and Broadcasting. New Delhi: Government of India, 1979.

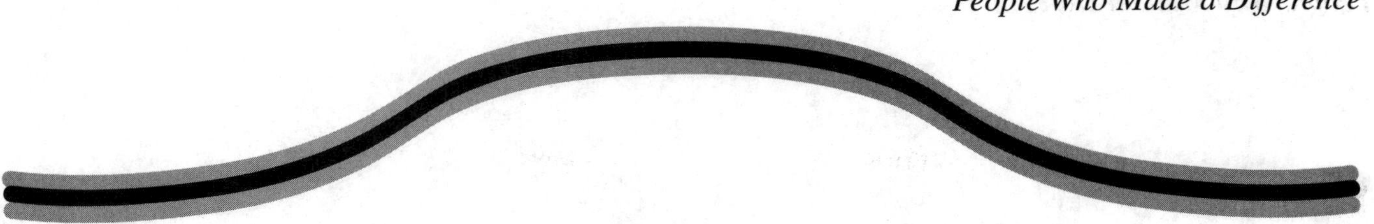

Mohandas Gandhi: A Man of Peaceful Action

1. Mohandas Gandhi received training to become a
   a. lawyer.
   b. vegetarian.
   c. religious leader.
   d. soldier.
2. Gandhi is called the Father of
   a. South Africa.
   b. Great Britian.
   c. India.
   d. Amritsar.
3. What did Albert Einstein mean by his remark at Gandhi's funeral?
   a. that no one would believe that Gandhi really existed
   b. that people would be amazed at how Gandhi never wavered in his stance against violence
   c. that Gandhi would be made into a Christian saint
   d. that Gandhi would quickly be forgotten
4. Gandhi changed his stance on non-violent protest after the Amritsar Massacre. True or False? Explain your answer.

   ____

   ____

   ____

5. Read Gandhi's speech carefully. What had the Indian nationalists been urging which prompted Gandhi's speech?

   ____

   ____

   ____

   ____

   ____

6. Would the world be a better place if today's world leaders followed Gandhi's non-violent policies? Defend your stance.

   ____

   ____

   ____

   ____

   ____

Amazing Courage: Irena Sendler's Silence

In September 1939 the Nazis invaded Poland. At that time Irena Sendler, 29, was a Catholic social worker in Warsaw. She saw the Nazis force 350,000 Jews into the Warsaw Ghetto. This area within the city was walled off and heavily guarded. The Jews had little access to food or medical care. And their only way out was to board a train that would carry them to their deaths in a gas chamber.

Irena joined Zegota, a secret group formed to help the Jews. She was chosen to find a way to take Jewish children from the Ghetto. She entered the Ghetto by telling the Germans that she had medicine for the people. Of course the Nazis did not care about the Jews getting the drugs. But they did not want diseases to spread to the rest of the city.

With the help of ten other Zegota members, Irena organized the secret removal of 2,500 children. Once out, the children went to orphanages, convents, and families. One of the hardest tasks Irena had was convincing the parents to give up their children. The parents did not know for sure that they would die. Many would not let them go. This was a terrible mistake, as less than 1 percent of the people in the Warsaw Ghetto survived the war.

To move the children, Irena had to be creative. She smuggled babies by sedating them and putting them into workers' toolboxes, sacks of potatoes, and under car seats. She had children crawl through sewer pipes with volunteers. Older kids memorized prayers so that they could "hide in the open" by appearing to be Christians. The people who received the children took a big risk. If discovered, the whole family could be killed.

Every day for 16 months Irena worked to save the children. She wrote each child's real and foster names on a paper. She hid it in a glass jar buried beneath a tree in a friend's backyard. When the war ended, she hoped the children could be found and their true identities revealed.

Then another Zegota member was tortured. She gave Irena's name. On October 20, 1943, the Gestapo seized Irena. These were the brutal Nazi police. They demanded that she tell the names of the other rescuers and where the children were placed. But she refused to speak. The Gestapo beat her. They broke both of her feet. Then they broke both of her legs. She was in unbearable pain. Still she refused to speak.

The Gestapo sent Irena to Pawiak Prison for execution. On the morning she was to die, she woke up glad! She knew that she only had to endure a few more hours without speaking. But a Zegota member had bribed the guard. He set her free and posted her name as executed. Zegota members hid her and nursed her back to health. Since this courageous woman did not get immediate medical treatment for her injuries, she had trouble walking for the rest of her life.

When Poland was freed in January 1945, Irena dug up the jar. But none of the children had living relatives with whom to reunite.

Amazing Courage: Irena Sendler's Silence

August 26, 1945

Dear Miss Sendler,

I want to thank you for taking me out of the Warsaw ghetto and giving me to my new family. My new parents are very nice to me. I have two sisters and a brother, too. But I still miss my parents. I wish they were alive. I want to be with them.

My new parents told me that you risked your life to save mine and that even when they beat you, you did not tell where I was. I can't believe how brave you are to save my life more than once. Thank you so much.

I also miss my religion. My new parents are Catholics, and we go to church each week. We do not celebrate Rosh Hashanah or Yom Kippur. I miss those celebrations. I remember my dad. I can still see him wearing his cap and praying. I miss my mom so much that I try not to think about her. When I do, I cry.

I know that you looked for my parents and grandparents and aunts and uncles and could find none of them. My new parents say they are probably dead and it's best to forget. I will try, but it is very hard. I wish things could be different.

Thanks again,

Marta (Goldstein) Zukoski

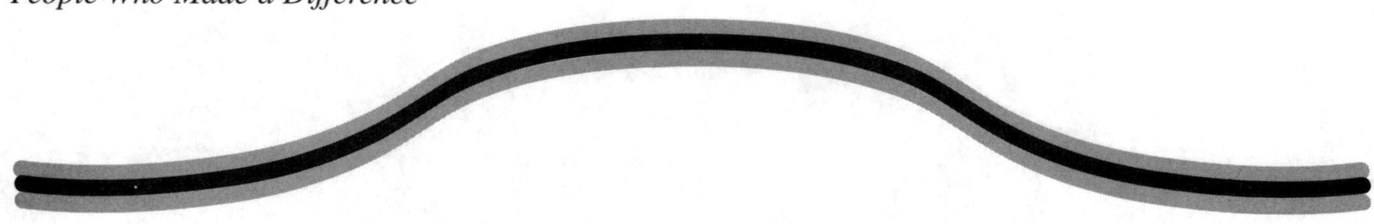

Amazing Courage: Irena Sendler's Silence

1. The Nazi police who broke Irena's feet and legs were called the
   a. Ghetto.
   b. Zegota.
   c. Pawiak.
   d. Gestapo.
2. Irena kept records on the children she saved because
   a. she knew that she would die and no one else would know the kids' identities.
   b. Zegota required her to do so.
   c. she hoped that the children would return to their parents after the war ended.
   d. she wanted to show the list to the newspapers and become famous.
3. After Irena escaped from prison, the police didn't look for her because they
   a. only searched for Jews.
   b. did not know that she was still alive.
   c. never looked for escaped prisoners.
   d. had lost interest in her and the children she rescued.
4. During the rescue operation, the most difficult part was getting parents to release their kids to Irena. True or False? Explain.

   ____

   ____

   ____

5. What is the tone of Marta's letter to Irena? Why is she writing to Irena? How do you know?

   ____

   ____

   ____

   ____

   ____

6. Would you have joined Zegota? Defend your stance.

   ____

   ____

   ____

   ____

   ____

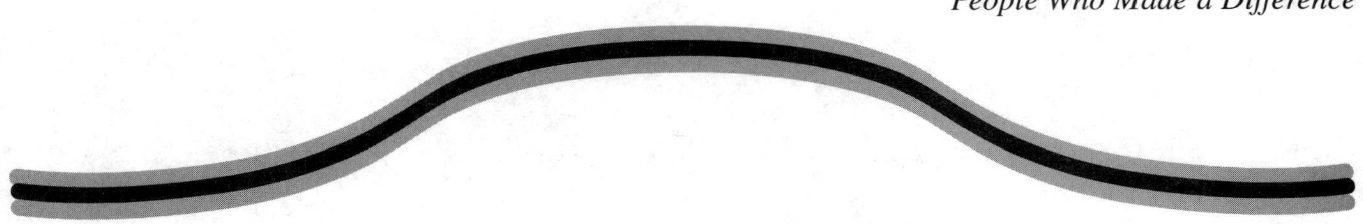

Thurgood Marshall, Supreme Court Justice

One of the most famous cases ever argued before the U.S. Supreme Court was . The Supreme Court is the highest court in America. And the decision it made on this case changed the whole education system in the United States. It spurred the movement to desegregate American society.

Courtesy of the Library of Congress, "Thurgood Marshall," LC-USZ62-60139

Before 1954, the policy had been "separate but equal" schools for whites and people of color. Even when children lived next door to a school, their skin color might make them go to a school miles away. What made this policy so bad was that the schools were not even close to equal. The schools with white students had more funds. They had better buildings, books, equipment, and buses. Schools for colored children were overcrowded, lacked books, and often had few buses.

Thurgood Marshall was an African-American lawyer. He argued this famous case before the Supreme Court with these words, "The only thing segregation can be is an inherent determination that the people who were formerly in slavery . . . shall be kept as near that stage as is possible. Now is the time . . . that the Court should make clear that that is not what our Constitution stands for." The Court agreed with his stirring words. In fact, every justice voted the same way. They ruled that separating children in public schools on the basis of race was wrong. It violated the Fourteenth Amendment, which requires that all citizens be treated equally. And it deprived minorities of equal educational opportunities. The Court decided that schools must be integrated.

Marshall presented a total of 19 cases before the U.S. Supreme Court. He won 14. Then, in 1967, he received an honor. He was appointed as a justice on the Supreme Court. First, President Lyndon Johnson chose him. Then the Senate had to agree that he was a good choice. Why? Justices are appointed for life. They cannot be removed unless they are impeached. They would have to do something seriously wrong to be impeached. The only other reason they may leave is if they choose to retire.

Marshall was the first African American to serve on the Court. As a justice, he upheld decisions allowing free expression and equal protection for the rights of the poor and minorities. He was also against capital punishment (the death penalty). By 1991 his health was failing. He retired from the Court and died in 1993.

Thurgood Marshall, Supreme Court Justice

In 1978 the U.S. Supreme Court ruled that race could be a factor in choosing a diverse student population in university admissions in *University of California v. Bakke*. However, quotas* in such affirmative action programs were wrong. The Court held that due to its 16 percent minority quota, the University had discriminated against Allan Bakke, a white applicant. His application had been rejected twice, although he had higher grades than some of the minority applicants granted admission. These are excerpts from Justice Thurgood Marshall's dissenting opinion:

"While I applaud the judgment of the Court that a university may consider race in its admissions process, it is more than a little ironic that, after several hundred years of class-based discrimination against Negroes, the Court is unwilling to hold that a class-based remedy for that discrimination is permissible. In declining to so hold, today's judgment ignores the fact that for several hundred years Negroes have been discriminated against, not as individuals, but rather solely because of the color of their skins. It is unnecessary in 20th-century America to have individual Negroes demonstrate that they have been victims of racial discrimination; the racism of our society has been so pervasive that none, regardless of wealth or position, has managed to escape its impact. The experience of Negroes in America has been different in kind, not just in degree, from that of other ethnic groups. It is not merely the history of slavery alone but also that a whole people were marked as inferior by the law. The dream of America as the great melting pot has not been realized for the Negro; because of his skin color he never even made it into the pot.

These differences in the experience of the Negro make it difficult for me to accept that Negroes cannot be afforded greater protection under the Fourteenth Amendment where it is necessary to remedy the effects of past discrimination . . . It is because of a legacy of unequal treatment that we now must permit the institutions of this society to give consideration to race in making decisions about who will hold the positions of influence, affluence, and prestige in America. For far too long, the doors to those positions have been shut to Negroes. If we are ever to become a fully integrated society, one in which the color of a person's skin will not determine the opportunities available to him or her, we must be willing to take steps to open those doors . . .

It has been said that this case involves only the individual, Bakke, and this University. I doubt, however, that there is a computer capable of determining the number of persons and institutions that may be affected by the decision in this case. I cannot even guess the number of state and local governments that have set up affirmative-action programs, which may be affected by today's decision. I fear that we have come full circle. After the Civil War our Government started several "affirmative action" programs. Then this Court in *Plessy v. Ferguson* destroyed the movement toward complete equality. For almost a century no action was taken, and this nonaction was with the approval of the courts. Then we had *Brown v. Board of Education* and the Civil Rights Acts of Congress, followed by numerous affirmative-action programs. Now, we have this Court again stepping in, this time to stop affirmative-action programs of the type used by the University of California."

*a fixed number of a group allowed to do something (be hired, be admitted, etc.)

Texas Civil Rights Review. "Thurgood Marshall in Bakke."

http://texascivilrightsreview.org/phpnuke/modules.php?name=News&file=article&sitd=129

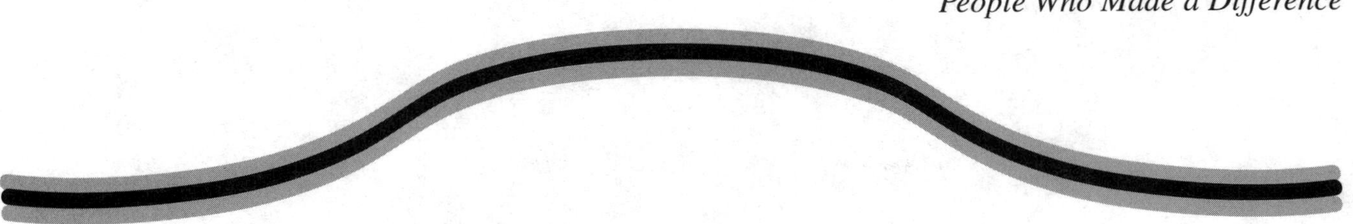

Thurgood Marshall, Supreme Court Justice

1. U.S. Supreme Court justices cannot leave the Court by
   a. being impeached.
   b. being fired by the president.
   c. retiring.
   d. dying.
2. What event happened last in Thurgood Marshall's life?
   a. Marshall wrote an opinion as a U.S. Supreme Court justice.
   b. Marshall learned to be a lawyer.
   c. Marshall argued *Brown v. the Board of Education of Topeka.*
   d. the Senate upheld President Johnson's choice for U.S. Supreme Court justice.
3. In 1954, Marshall convinced the U.S. Supreme Court that
   a. it should reverse its position on the *University of California v. Bakke.*
   b. quotas for minority students in higher education were not a good idea.
   c. separate schools were holding back minority children.
   d. separate schools were helping minority children to succeed.
4. Marshall agreed with the U.S. Supreme Court's ruling in *University of California v. Bakke.* True or False? Explain.

____

____

____

5. Describe what an affirmative action program is and what its goal is. You may need to reread Marshall's opinion in the *University of California v. Bakke.*

____

____

____

____

____

6. Do you agree with Marshall's opinion in the *University of California v. Bakke*? Defend your stance.

____

____

____

____

____

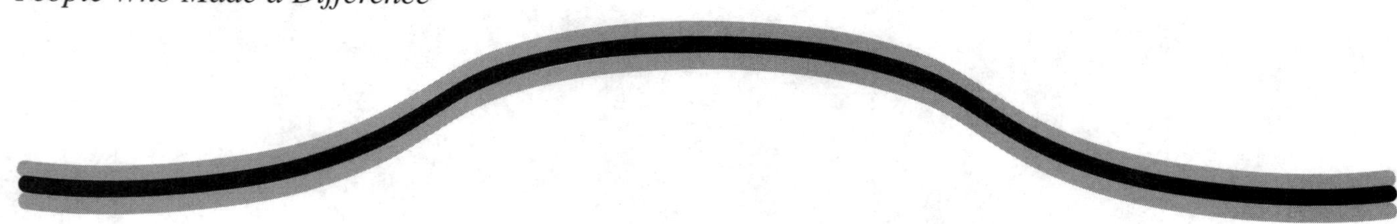

Mother Teresa:

Greatest Humanitarian of the Twentieth Century

An amazing woman died in September 1997. She owned two garments, a bucket for washing, a sleeping mat, a Bible, and less than $1. Yet she was admired around the world. Why? She was the greatest humanitarian of the twentieth century (1900s).

Mother Teresa was born Agnes Bojaxhui in 1910 in what is now Macedonia. By the age of 12 she knew that she wanted to be a Roman Catholic nun. She joined the Order of Loreto at 18. She took the name Teresa in honor of Saint Teresa and used it for the rest of her life.

She went to India and taught in a convent school for rich children in Calcutta, the capital city. When she became the principal, she received the title of Mother Teresa. The horrible slum conditions just outside her bedroom window bothered her. On September 10, 1946, she heard God's call. He told her to leave the convent and live among the "poorest of the poor" and help them however she could. Mother Teresa immediately asked to do this. But the Order did not let her go until 1948. She left the convent with no place to go and just a few coins. She lived on the streets with the homeless. Then a person offered to let her sleep in an attic.

In December 1948 she started a school out on a street. The next year three of her former students joined her. By 1950 she had enough sisters to form a new religious order. She named it the Missionary Sisters of Charity. Two years later Mother Teresa convinced city officials to give her some unused rooms. There she made a home for the dying. She and her sisters carried ill people from the gutters. They washed them and gave them medical care. They offered the last rites of whatever religion the patient believed in. In 1953 Mother Teresa set up a home for orphans and abandoned children. Then she opened a place for lepers in 1957. People with this dreaded disease can lose their limbs. Although the nun never earned a cent, she always managed to have the funds she needed within 24 hours of needing them!

Many men wanted to assist in her work. So the Missionary Brothers of Charity formed in 1963. Soon more orders of the Missionaries of Charity formed. They cared for the poor and sick in nations all over the world. By the end of the 20th century more than 150 such missions helped those in need.

In 1979, Mother Teresa received the Nobel Peace Prize. She donated the $990,000 that came with the award to the poor. The United States honored her with the Presidential Medal of Freedom in 1985 and a Congressional Medal of Honor in 1997.

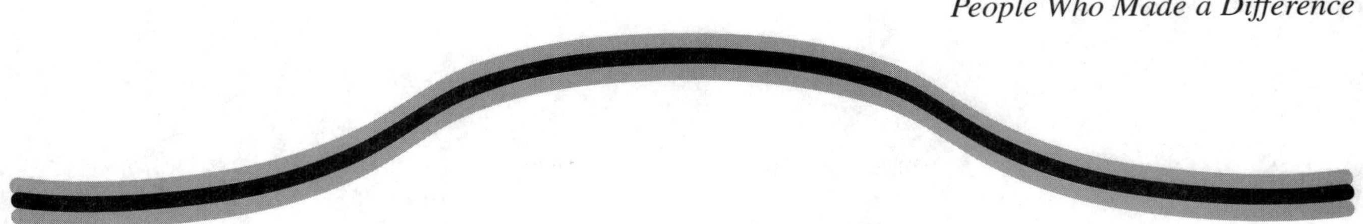

Mother Teresa:

Greatest Humanitarian of the Twentieth Century

Here are excerpts from Mother Teresa's Nobel Peace Prize acceptance speech given December 11, 1979:

"The poor are very wonderful people. One evening we went out and we picked up four people from the street. And one of them was in a most terrible condition—and I told the Sisters: You take care of the other three, I will take care of this one that looked worse. So I did for her all that my love can do. I put her in bed, and there was such a beautiful smile on her face. She took hold of my hand, as she said one word only: Thank you—and she died.

I could not help but examine my conscience before her, and I asked what would I say if I was in her place. And my answer was very simple. I would have tried to draw a little attention to myself, I would have said I am hungry, that I am dying, I am cold, I am in pain, or something, but she gave me much more—she gave me her grateful love. And she died with a smile on her face.

As that man whom we picked up from the drain, half eaten with worms, and we brought him to the home. [He said,] "I have lived like an animal in the street, but I am going to die like an angel, loved and cared for." And it was so wonderful to see the greatness of that man who could speak like that, who could die like that without blaming anybody, without cursing anybody, without comparing anything. Like an angel—this is the greatness of our people.

Some time ago in Calcutta we had great difficulty in getting sugar, and I don't know how the word got around to the children, and a little boy of four years old, Hindu boy, went home and told his parents: I will not eat sugar for three days, I will give my sugar to Mother Teresa for her children. After three days his father and mother brought him to our home. I had never met them before, and this little one could scarcely pronounce my name, but he knew exactly what he had come to do. He knew that he wanted to share his love."

Nobel Prize Organization. "Mother Teresa Nobel Lecture, 11 December, 1979."

http://nobelprize.virtual.museum/nobel_prizes/peace/laureates/1979/teresa-lecture.html

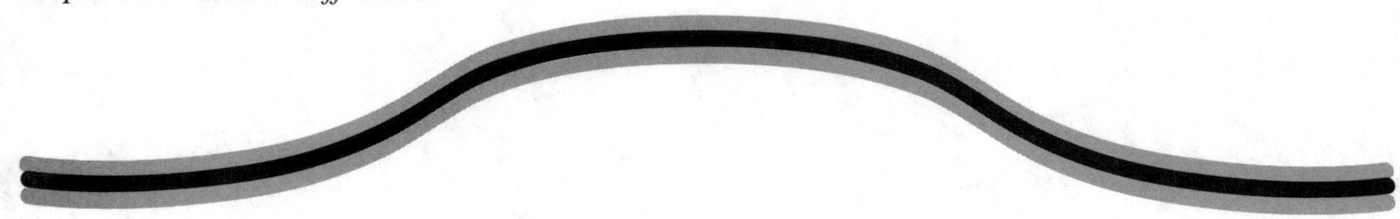

Mother Teresa:

Greatest Humanitarian of the Twentieth Century

1. As a child, Mother Teresa lived in
   a. Bojaxhui.
   b. Calcutta.
   c. Macedonia.
   d. the United States.
2. The word means someone who
   a. takes action to improve the welfare of others.
   b. is a Roman Catholic nun in India.
   c. works as a nurse.
   d. joins a Missionary of Charity order.
3. Why did the United States honor Mother Teresa with two medals?
   a. because she needed the $990,000 that came with the awards
   b. because she was the most charitable U.S. citizen
   c. because she helped to prevent a war between the United States and India
   d. because she was a woman who worked tirelessly to help others
4. Mother Teresa was impressed by the attitude of the dying people that she had met. True or False? Explain.

____

____

____

5. Why do you think Mother Teresa chose to talk about the people of India in her Nobel Peace Prize acceptance speech?

____

____

____

____

____

6. Of the three people's stories that Mother Teresa mentioned, which did you find the most moving? Why?

____

____

____

____

____

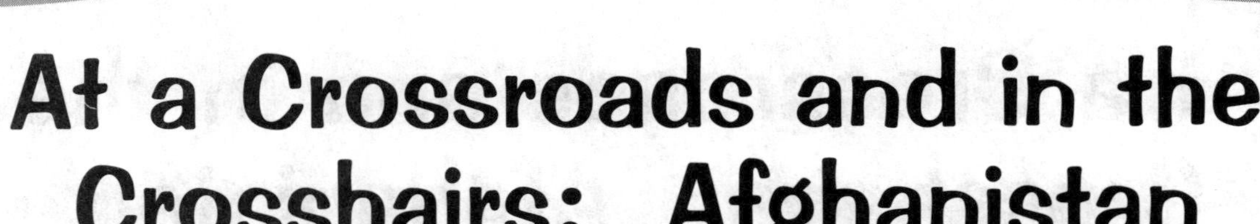

At a Crossroads and in the Crosshairs: Afghanistan

Afghanistan is a nation in the Middle East. It is landlocked and has no seashore. This gives it very cold winters and hot, dry summers. If it were near a body of water, its climate would be less extreme. This nation has a long history of warfare and conquest. Why? It is the crossroads of several ancient Asian trade routes. Over the years the Persians, Greeks, Mongols, British, and Russians have invaded. In fact, more than two million Afghans are refugees. They no longer live in their homeland. From 1979 to 1989 there was a Soviet invasion. It was followed by a four-year civil war. More than one million people died. Five million left the country. They went to Pakistan and Iran (formerly Persia).

The many wars have caused major problems for Afghans. Only 36 percent of adults know how to read and write. There are not enough schools or teachers for all the nation's children. And in some places, girls cannot go to school even if one is available. Also, Afghanistan is one of the world's least-developed nations. Farmers till and harvest using old-fashioned tools and methods that other countries abandoned a century ago. Families live in small homes made of sun-dried mud bricks. Most do not have running water or electricity. Some Afghans are nomads. They move from one place to another to ensure that their sheep or goats have good grazing land. They live in tents made of goat hair.

Following the terrorist attacks on September 11, 2001, the United States took military action against this nation's leaders. The Taliban were removed because they protected Osama bin Laden. He had masterminded the attacks against America. After the Taliban were defeated, a constitution was written. A presidential election was held in 2004. National Assembly elections occurred in 2005. For the first time in its history, Afghanistan is a democratic nation. However, Afghans do not have all the freedoms that Americans do. Islam is the state religion. A person can receive the death penalty for switching to a different religion. And some Afghan groups will not let a woman leave her home unless a male relative goes with her.

Those who believe in Islam are called Muslims. In Afghanistan there are two major groups. They are the Sunnis and the Shiites. Each group interprets Islamic law differently. So there is often fighting between the groups. About 80 percent of Afghans are Sunni.

At a Crossroads and in the Crosshairs: Afghanistan

Major Branches of Islam

Sunni
(940 million worldwide)

- Allah has a body and can be seen on Earth and in the afterlife.
- Allah can command a person to kill another, making the act good.
- Allah does some things randomly.
- Allah creates all people's acts.
- Must pray with head on a mat five times a day.
- No fixed-term temporary marriages.
- Woman may have bare heads, drive, work outside the home, and participate in the government and army.

Both

- Allah is the only God.
- Mohammed is his last prophet.
- Allah will resurrect all humans and question their actions.
- Murder, adultery, and rape are sins.
- Five pillars of Islam.
- Quran is the holy book.
- Cannot make images of Allah or humans

Shiites
(120 million worldwide)

- Allah has no body and can never be seen.
- Allah can only command good things.
- Allah has a purpose in all that He does.
- Allah knows what we will do but doesn't make us do it.
- Must pray with head on hard clay three to five times a day.
- Allow fixed-term temporary marriages.
- Women must stay entirely covered and cannot leave home without a male relative

At a Crossroads and in the Crosshairs: Afghanistan

1. Most Afghans do not have
   a. an education.
   b. food.
   c. clothing.
   d. shelter.
2. Persia was the former name of the country of
   a. Afghanistan.
   b. Iran.
   c. Islam.
   d. Pakistan.
3. One right Afghans do not have that Americans do have is
   a. freedom of speech.
   b. the ability to elect leaders.
   c. religious choice.
   d. the right to bear arms (carry guns).
4. Both Sunni and Shiite Muslims believe Allah is the only God and Mohammed is His Prophet. True or False? Explain.

   ____

   ____

   ____

5. Describe the two differences in beliefs that probably cause the strongest disagreements between Sunnis and Shiites. Why did you choose those factors?

   ____

   ____

   ____

   ____

   ____

6. If Afghanistan did not have a state religion, would fighting between the Sunnis and the Shiites decrease? Defend your stance.

   ____

   ____

   ____

   ____

   ____

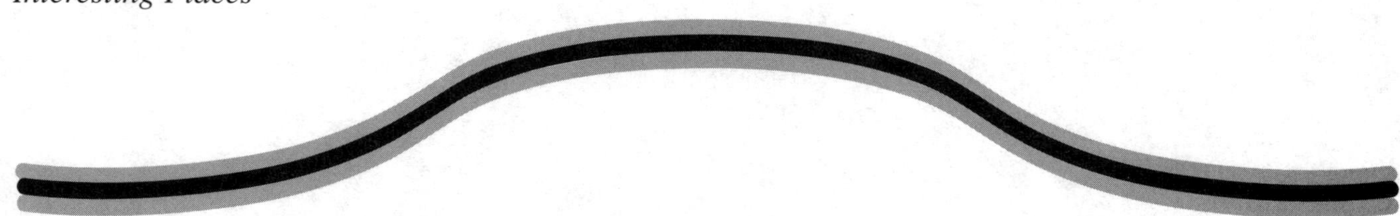

Antarctica: A Hidden Land

Despite its snow and ice, Antarctica is the driest continent on Earth. It is a polar desert. Only one to two inches of snow falls each year. In some of its dry valleys it has not rained for over two million years. Falling snow evaporates before it hits the ground, and the air is so dry that nothing decays. As a result, seal carcasses over 1,000 years old lie in these valleys!

Antarctica is the coldest place on Earth. The lowest temperature ever recorded occurred there in 1983. It was -128.6°F! By contrast, the Arctic Circle's coldest temperature is -90°F. Why is Antarctica colder than the Arctic? Continents surround the polar ice cap in the Arctic. They give off stored heat. This warms the Arctic Ocean. Antarctica is a continent surrounded by a vast ocean. And its icy blanket reflects 80 percent of the sunlight that falls on it. In fact, the temperature in Antarctica almost never rises above 32°F. Strong, cold winds often whip across its surface.

Yet millions of years ago, Antarctica had trees, small mammals, and even dinosaurs. It was a warm place! Scientists know this from fossils found there. They theorize that the continent broke free of a huge supercontinent. It slowly drifted south to its current location. Glaciers formed there about 38 million years ago.

Even now Antarctica supports life. Some patches of Antarctic lichen are over 1,000 years old. Most of the fish living in the Southern Ocean have a chemical in their blood. It acts like the antifreeze in a car's radiator. It keeps their bodies from freezing even though the water temperature is 28.7° F—slightly warmer than the temperature at which saltwater freezes. Small plants and algae also live in the water. Penguins and the sea lions that eat them call Antarctica home, too.

Antarctica is twice the size of Australia. But only two percent of its land is exposed. The rest is covered with ice. More than 90 percent of Earth's permanent ice is there. It built up over countless years from snow that never melted. This huge ice sheet not only covers the whole continent, it holds 68 percent of the world's freshwater! Hidden 2.5 miles below the ice lies the world's largest, deepest, freshwater lake. Lake Vostok was discovered during the 1970s. Scientists believe that it covers more than 5,400 square miles.

Twelve nations signed the Antarctic Treaty in 1959. In it they agreed to use Antarctica for research and share the knowledge gained. Now scientists live there year-round in research stations. Ships must steer around icebergs—some the size of Rhode Island—to bring them supplies. The planes that deliver people or supplies take off and land on runways of solid ice.

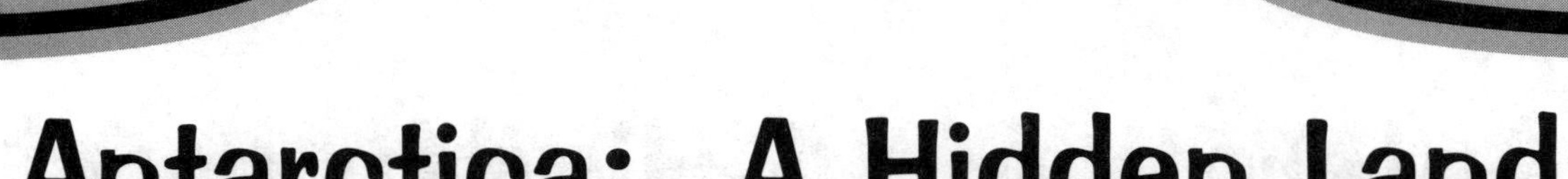

Antarctica: A Hidden Land

A British man named Robert Scott led a group of men to the South Pole. They arrived on January 17, 1912, only to find that a Norwegian team had beaten them one month before. The men turned back toward their base camp. But they never arrived. Here are excerpts from the actual journal of Scott found on his body by a search party on November 12, 1912:

"FRIDAY, MARCH 16 OR SATURDAY 17—LOST TRACK OF DATES, BUT THINK THE LAST CORRECT. TRAGEDY ALL ALONG THE LINE. AT LUNCH, THE DAY BEFORE YESTERDAY, POOR TITUS OATES SAID HE COULDN'T GO ON; HE PROPOSED WE SHOULD LEAVE HIM IN HIS SLEEPING-BAG. THAT WE COULD NOT DO, AND WE INDUCED HIM TO COME ON, ON THE AFTERNOON MARCH. IN SPITE OF ITS AWFUL NATURE FOR HIM HE STRUGGLED ON AND WE MADE A FEW MILES. AT NIGHT HE WAS WORSE AND WE KNEW THE END HAD COME. SHOULD THIS BE FOUND I WANT THESE FACTS RECORDED. OATES' LAST THOUGHTS WERE OF HIS MOTHER, BUT IMMEDIATELY BEFORE HE TOOK PRIDE IN THINKING THAT HIS REGIMENT WOULD BE PLEASED WITH THE BOLD WAY IN WHICH HE MET HIS DEATH. WE CAN TESTIFY TO HIS BRAVERY. HE HAS BORNE INTENSE SUFFERING FOR WEEKS WITHOUT COMPLAINT . . . HE DID NOT--WOULD NOT--GIVE UP HOPE TILL THE VERY END. HE WAS A BRAVE SOUL. THIS WAS THE END. HE SLEPT THROUGH THE NIGHT BEFORE LAST, HOPING NOT TO WAKE; BUT HE WOKE IN THE MORNING - YESTERDAY. IT WAS BLOWING A BLIZZARD. HE SAID, 'I AM JUST GOING OUTSIDE AND MAY BE SOME TIME.' HE WENT OUT INTO THE BLIZZARD, AND WE HAVE NOT SEEN HIM SINCE."

WEDNESDAY, MARCH 21—GOT WITHIN 11 MILES OF DEPOT* MONDAY NIGHT; HAD TO LAY UP ALL YESTERDAY IN SEVERE BLIZZARD. TODAY FORLORN HOPE, WILSON AND BOWERS GOING TO DEPOT FOR FUEL.

THURSDAY, MARCH 22 AND 23—BLIZZARD BAD AS EVER—WILSON AND BOWERS UNABLE TO START—TOMORROW LAST CHANCE—NO FUEL AND ONLY ONE OR TWO OF FOOD LEFT—MUST BE NEAR THE END. HAVE DECIDED IT SHALL BE NATURAL—WE SHALL MARCH FOR THE DEPOT WITH OR WITHOUT OUR EFFECTS AND DIE IN OUR TRACKS.

THURSDAY, MARCH 29—SINCE THE 21ST WE HAVE HAD A CONTINUOUS GALE. WE HAD FUEL TO MAKE TWO CUPS OF TEA APIECE AND BARE FOOD FOR TWO DAYS ON THE 20TH. EVERY DAY WE HAVE BEEN READY TO START FOR OUR DEPOT 11 MILES AWAY, BUT OUTSIDE THE DOOR OF THE TENT IT REMAINS A SCENE OF WHIRLING DRIFT. I DO NOT THINK WE CAN HOPE FOR ANY BETTER THINGS NOW. WE SHALL STICK IT OUT TO THE END, BUT WE ARE GETTING WEAKER, OF COURSE, AND THE END CANNOT BE FAR. IT SEEMS A PITY, BUT I DO NOT THINK I CAN WRITE MORE.

R. SCOTT"

*place where supplies are stored

Eyewitness to History. "Doomed Expedition to the South Pole, 1912." **http://www.eyewitnesstohistory.com/scott.htm,**

Antarctica: A Hidden Land

1. What amount of Antarctica's land is hidden beneath ice?

a. 2 percent
b. 38 percent
c. 90 percent
d. 98 percent

2. Which continent is half the size of Antarctica?

a. Australia
b. Europe
c. Africa
d. Asia

3. Antarctica is a polar desert, yet Robert Scott refers to an unending blizzard. Why?

a. It was freak weather that caused heavy snowfall.
b. High winds blow around loose snow that's on the ground, so it looks like a blizzard.
c. Scott was hallucinating because he was dying.
d. Scott did not know what a blizzard was.

4. The Arctic Circle does not get as cold as Antarctica because it is surrounded by water. True or False? Explain your answer.

____

____

____

5. Was Robert Scott impressed with the way that Titus Oates met his death?

____

____

____

____

____

6. Scott and his men were found dead inside their tent. Should they have braved the blizzard and tried to reach the depot before they began running out of food and fuel? Defend your stance.

____

____

____

____

____

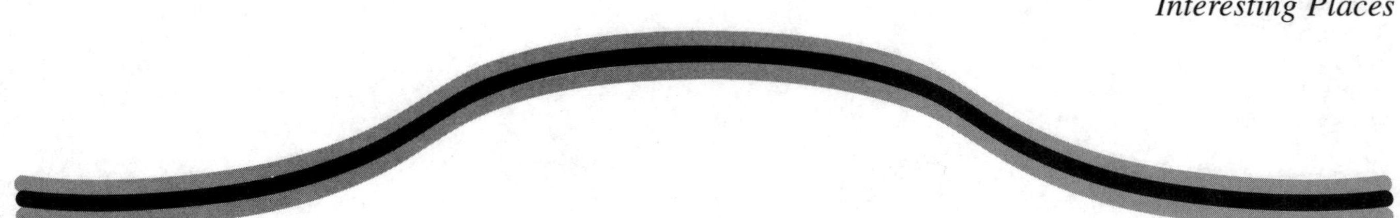

The Land Down Under: Australia

Australia is the only nation that is also a continent. It lies between the South Pacific Ocean and the Indian Ocean. Dark-skinned aborigines have lived there for at least 40,000 years. But whites, who make up most of today's population, first came in 1788. They were prisoners. Great Britain had exiled them. Most had committed small crimes. Others had just been unable to pay their bills.

In 1851 gold was found in Australia. For the next ten years, people rushed there. They hoped to make a fortune. The population nearly tripled. Most miners did not find enough gold to buy their ticket home. They had to stay. Meanwhile convicts kept arriving. They came until 1868. A total of more than 160,000 were sent.

Great Britain owned Australia as a group of colonies. In 1890 it granted these colonies their freedom. The former colonies decided to join together as one nation. They became the six states of the Commonwealth of Australia in 1901.

Australia has a sunny climate and large, open spaces. It is the second driest continent. Only Antarctica gets less precipitation. However, there are places with enough rainfall and good soil to grow crops. The nation is famous for its unusual wildlife. Many species of plants and animals live there and nowhere else on Earth.

Australia's northern territory has one of the most extreme environments on Earth. Half of the year it rains all the time. Everything floods. Then, for the next six months, there is no rain. Everything dries up. Wildfires rage through the area. In the summer, it often reaches 113 degrees F.

Australia has the world's longest fence. It encloses one-third of the nation to keep dingoes (wild dogs) from killing cattle and sheep. The country is the world's top producer and exporter of wool. It also mines the most bauxite, the ore used to make aluminum.

At the end of World War II in 1945, a program encouraged people from the war-torn areas of Europe to move to Australia. The population grew rapidly. Now most of the people live along the southeastern coast. Like Canada, its government is a constitutional monarchy. The monarch of England is the head of state. But the monarch does not run the government. An elected prime minister does that.

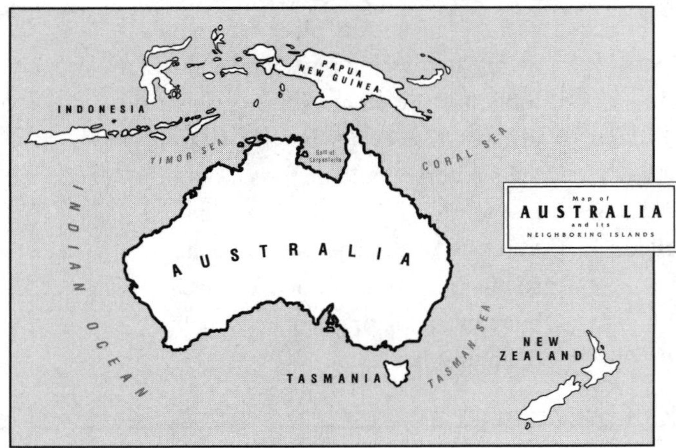

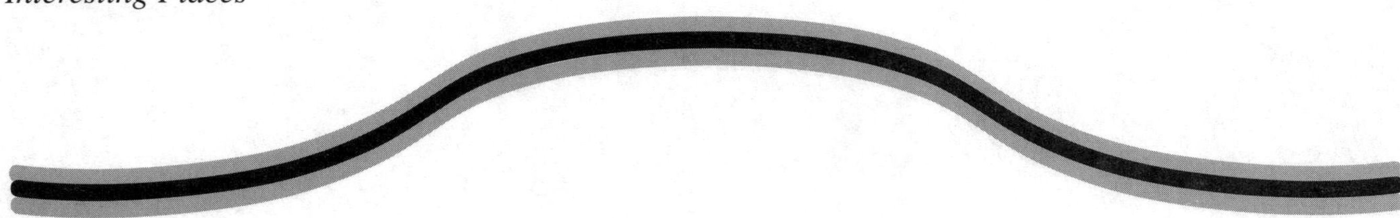

The Land Down Under: Australia

Victoria Daily News July 16, 2008

Are Koalas Causing Trouble on Kangaroo Island?

AWA says koalas not to blame for island's problems

Thousands of trees are dying on Kangaroo Island, and the Australian Wildlife Association (AWA) says that disease is to blame. Edward Archer, AWA chief, said that in 1994 the fungus Phytophthera was identified on the island. This fungus caused Sudden Oak Death Syndrome in Big Sur, California, in the United States. Scientists do not yet know why it develops in patches or why some tree species catch it and others do not.

The people living on Kangaroo Island say that there are too many koalas, and they are destroying the trees. They favor "culling"—a nice term for killing—the koalas. The AWA opposes killing koalas, especially since there are less than 100,000 left in the nation. The fur trade made these animals extinct in South Australia in the 1920s. They were reintroduced, and many thrived on Kangaroo Island until recently. Now food shortages are causing increased competition. The Federal Minister for the Environment has assured the public that the koalas on Kangaroo Island won't be culled.

Everyone agrees that there is a problem and that Kangaroo Island koalas will soon face starvation. But the AWA maintains that there are too few trees rather than too many koalas. Overgrazing by koalas has been blamed for the death of eucalyptus as well. The AWA claims that there are other factors working against native vegetation, including Phytophthera, insects, logging, and environmental degradation by humans. Archer said, "Most of Kangaroo Island is grazed by sheep. As tree saplings sprout, the sheep eat them. New trees do not have a chance to grow. Add to that wildfires, wild pigs, and a lack of good fencing. How can anyone blame the koalas for those things?"

People have suggested relocating the koalas to the mainland. But relocating could be just a "soft cull." The animals would die anyway. It would just take longer and be less obvious. Why? Koalas live in social groups. Any place they would be released would put social and food pressure on already-existing groups. Koalas newly released into the territory would be forced out of that territory. One of the best places to release the koalas would be the southeast forests of South Australia, but current logging practices make them unsuitable.

Others have suggested selling the animals to zoos (currently against international law) or spaying or neutering koala babies. The AWA has recommended that the Bureau of the Environment start a tree planting program on the island, including fencing the areas so that the new saplings can grow without disturbance from any animals. Yet even the AWA admits that this isn't a complete solution. Archer stated, "Planting more trees is just a starting point. There is no quick-fix. These complex problems will require long-term thinking and consensus among botany and wildlife experts."

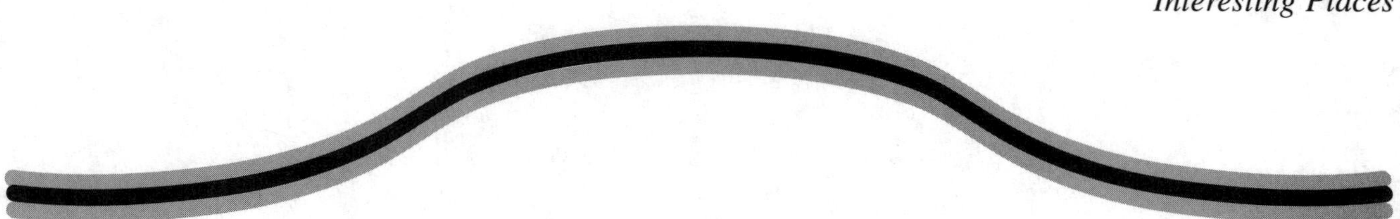

The Land Down Under: Australia

1. Gold was found in Australia in
   - a. 1788.
   - b. 1851.
   - c. 1868.
   - d. 1901.
2. The ancestors of most of the people living in Australia today came from
   - a. North America.
   - b. Asia.
   - c. Africa.
   - d. Europe.
3. The animals that survive in Australia's northern territory are able to live in very
   - a. wet and very dry conditions.
   - b. wet conditions only.
   - c. dry conditions only.
   - d. hot and very cold conditions.
4. Australia gets less rainfall than Africa. True or False? Explain.

   ____

   ____

   ____

5. What are the four possible reasons for the lack of trees on Kangaroo Island? Describe each one.

   ____

   ____

   ____

   ____

   ____

6. What should be done with the koalas on Kangaroo Island? Defend your stance.

   ____

   ____

   ____

   ____

   ____

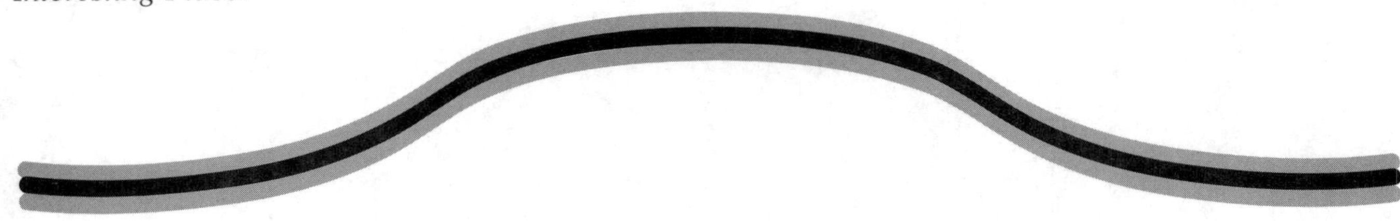

Bulgaria: A Balkan Nation

Bulgaria is one of the countries called the Balkans. These countries lie on the Balkan Peninsula in southeastern Europe. Four seas surround this peninsula. This nation is over 1,320 years old. During that time it was conquered by Alexander the Great, ruled by tzars and kings, and made a part of the Soviet Union. In 1990 the first free elections were held. Today the nation is a democracy. However, it is considered a developing nation. Its people have one of the lowest standards of living in Europe. Wages are low. Yet food, housing, and furniture cost a lot. Few people can afford a car. The nation is still struggling to reach economic balance after the damage done by almost 40 years of Communist rule.

Mountains cover most of Bulgaria. Although the nation has 490 rivers, not one of them is navigable! However, boats can go on the Danube River, which separates this nation from Romania. Bulgaria is an agricultural country. More than half of its land is devoted to farming. One of the biggest crops is sunflowers, which have seeds full of fat and protein. They can be fed to chickens and pigs or used to make cooking oil or margarine. Every part of the sunflower plant is used. The stalks grow nearly 10 feet tall. They are chopped into fodder for cattle, horses, and sheep to chew. A variety of other fruits, grains, and vegetables are also grown.

During World War II, Bulgaria was an ally of Germany. This means that the nation promised not to fight the German military. But when Germany demanded that the nation hand over its 50,000 Jews, King Boris III refused. He knew that the Jews would be sent to concentration camps where they would probably die. Bulgarian church leaders and others said that they would lie on the railroad tracks to stop the deportation trains. Germany decided not to pursue the matter. Every Bulgarian Jew was saved.

Today Bulgaria boasts a 99 percent literacy rate. That means that just one percent of its people cannot read or write. After eighth grade, students must take an exam to get into their chosen high school. Some students select a vocational high school in order to learn a trade in three years. But those who choose vocational training cannot go to college.

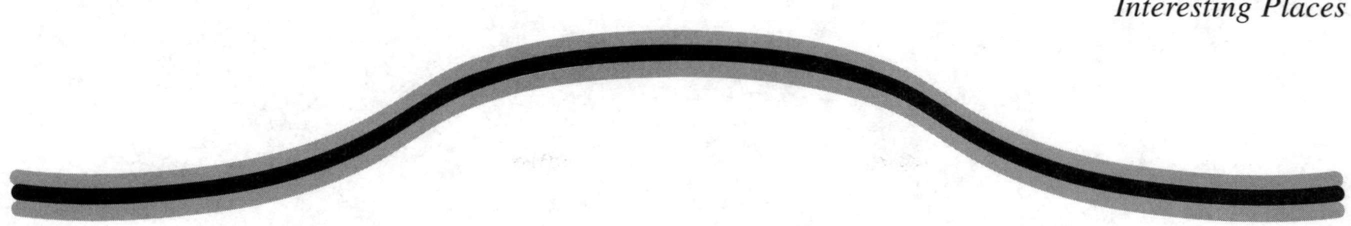

Bulgaria: A Balkan Nation

In 1941 Adolf-Heniz Beckerle was the German ambassador to Sofia, Bulgaria. He sent the following telegram to Nazi headquarters:

> The Bulgarians live with Armenians, Greeks, and Gypsies. They do not find any disadvantages to living with the Jews. They would view as suspicious measures being taken against the Jews. They do not appear to be willing to cooperate in the deportation of that population.
>
> The government has informed me of the fact that the Jews played a positive role in the Balkan wars, which freed Bulgaria from its long Ottoman Turkish domination. Bulgarian Jews are not rich, although they are represented in the professions and the arts. There are no Jewish ghettos in this nation.
>
> I have noticed that Jews are suppliers, physicians, and dentists for the Royal Court. I intercepted a message sent by the king to the IX Bulgarian Zionist Conference that read, "My best regards to the Bulgarian Zionists who always have been good citizens." The Jewish Consistory in Sofia and the king regularly exchange congratulations on holidays and anniversaries.
>
> There are even rumors that King Boris III has said, "German treatment of the Jews is inhuman."
>
> There is a situation developing here. I await your orders.
>
> Adolf Beckerle

Balkan Info. "The Rescue of the Bulgarian Jews."
http://www.b-info.com/places/Bulgaria/Jewish/jul12.shtml

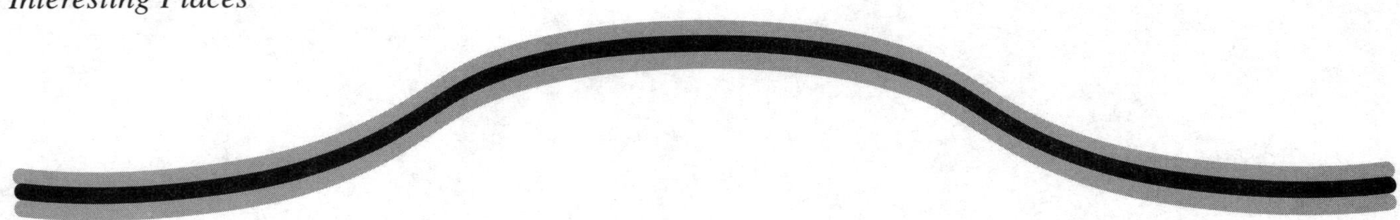

Bulgaria: A Balkan Nation

1. If a male Bulgarian student selects a vocational high school, he can

a. become wealthy rapidly.

b. choose to go to college.

c. not go on to college.

d. skip learning to read and write.

2. Ships can travel on how many of Bulgaria's many rivers?

a. all

b. on half

c. three

d. none

3. During World War II, Germany did not invade Bulgaria because Bulgaria

a. handed over all its Jews without a fight.

b. was allied with Germany.

c. threatened to bomb Germany's capital.

d. had such a strong army.

4. Bulgaria's economy is weak. True or False? Explain.

____

____

____

5. What was the purpose of Adolf Beckerle's telegram to Nazi headquarters?

____

____

____

____

____

6. Do you think that Bulgaria's policies about high school are wise? Defend your stance.

____

____

____

____

____

The Cradle of Civilization: Iraq

Sumer, the world's first known civilization, developed in what is now Iraq. The Sumerians lived there between 3500 and 3000 B.C. They had a mathematical system based on the number 60. They created the 60-minute hour we use. They made the first plow and possibly the first wheel.

Sumerians may have had the world's first system of writing. They carved marks into wet clay tablets. We call these marks cuneiform. The system spread all over southwestern Asia. Many of these tablets still exist. People have learned about ancient societies from them.

The Sumerians had sun-dried mud brick buildings. These bricks do not last forever. So no complete example of their architecture still stands. But some ruins do, and from them people have figured out what the original buildings probably looked like.

Ancient Iraq was called Mesopotamia. Later it was part of the Arab Empire. After World War I it separated from Turkish rule. It gained full independence in 1932. The discovery of vast oil reserves made the nation's future look bright.

The Iraqi people's standard of living rose between 1950 and the 1970s. But then a brutal leader, Saddam Hussein, came to power in 1979. He invaded neighboring Iran. This led to an eight-year war. Iraq lost. But that didn't stop Hussein. He used banned chemical weapons to kill Iranians and even thousands of his own citizens! He killed the Kurds, a non-Arab minority group in Iraq. Then he had his troops invade Kuwait. This time the United States fought back in the Persian Gulf War of 1991. Iraq lost again.

The United States suspected that Iraq had weapons of mass destruction. It also thought that the nation harbored members of al-Qaeda. This terrorist group attacked America in September 2001 and killed thousands. U.S. troops went to Iraq. They removed Hussein from power in 2003. Americans hope that Iraq will become a successful democracy.

Currently just 40 percent of Iraqi adults can read and write. The new government wants to improve people's lives through education. Now all children ages 6 through 12 must go to school.

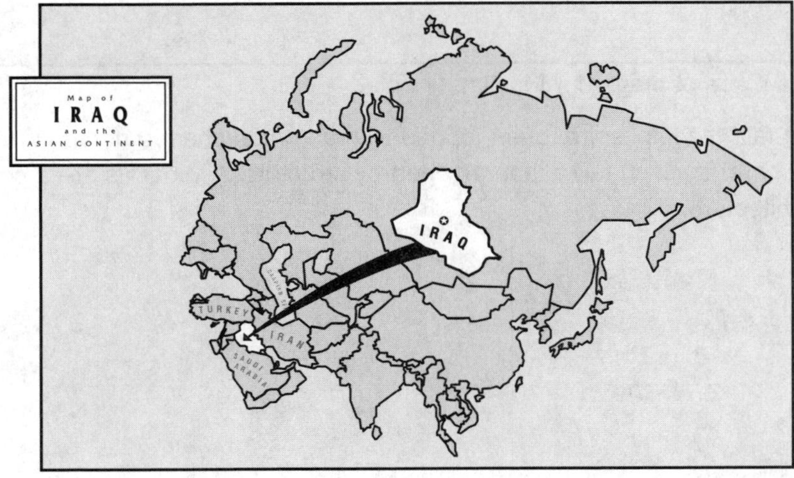

The Cradle of Civilization: Iraq

All About Islam | Islamic Architecture

The Great Mosque[1] in Samarra, Iraq, is believed to have been started in 820 A.D. It was finished by 851. At that time it was the largest mosque on Earth. Made of baked brick, this beautiful example of Islamic architecture features a 164-foot spiral minaret.[2]

Samarra is on the Tigris River, about 78 miles north of Baghdad, the capital of Iraq.

[1]A mosque is a place of prayer for Muslims.

[2]A minaret is a tall, graceful spire, often topped with an onion-shaped dome. When free-standing, a minaret is much taller than any nearby structures. Minarets are a common part of Islamic architecture.

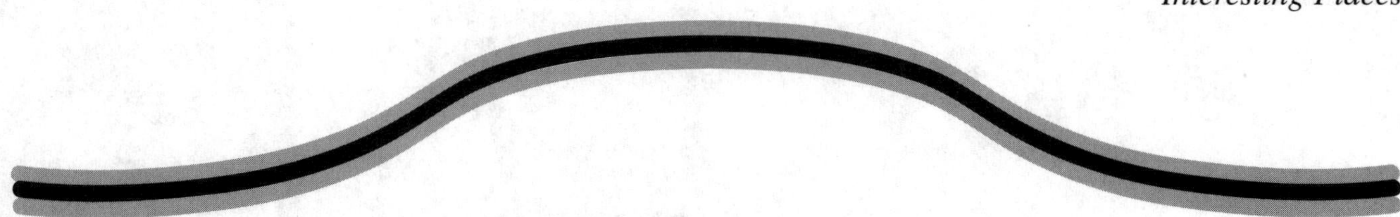

The Cradle of Civilization: Iraq

1. A cuneiform is a kind of
   a. sun-dried mud brick
   b. mathematical system.
   c. calendar.
   d. writing.
2. The Iraqi people's standard of living improved after
   a. oil was found beneath their land.
   b. Saddam Hussein came to power.
   c. their army invaded Kuwait.
   d. the Turks seized control of the nation.
3. Which is the name of one of Iraq's rivers?
   a. Kurds
   b. Sumerian
   c. Mesopotamia
   d. Tigris
4. Examples of Islamic architecture can be found in Iraq. True or False? Explain.

   ____

5. What does the Great Mosque tell us about Iraqis of the past?

   ____

6. Did the United States do the right thing by invading Iraq in 2003? Defend your stance.

   ____

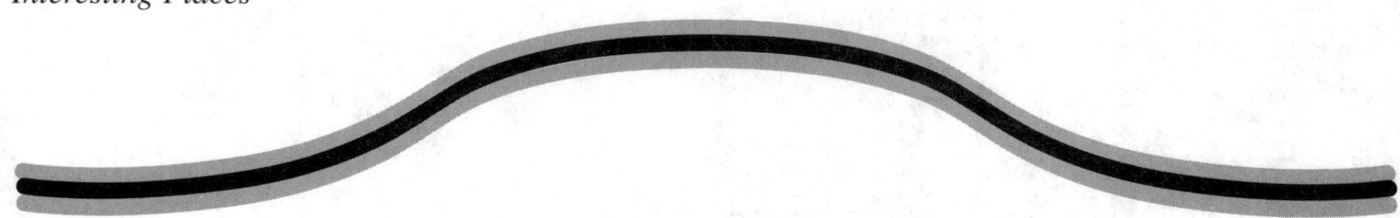

Jamaica, Jewel in the Caribbean Sea

Paradise. That's what tourists call Jamaica. The island nation has beautiful mountains. Its entire shoreline has white sand beaches. Its mild climate and gorgeous scenery draw many visitors each year. Some come to snorkel and scuba dive in the marine parks. These parks have beautiful coral reefs. The water is so clear that sunlight reaches to a depth of 80 feet! But swimmers must steer clear of the Portuguese man-of-war. This creature has a translucent balloon-like organ called a float. Below the float lies tentacles up to 165 feet long. Each one has hundreds of stingers. The sting is painful and can cause bad reactions in people.

Christopher Columbus landed in Jamaica in 1494. The first Spanish colony was set up in 1509. It began a terrible time for the gentle natives on the island. Half of them were dead by 1598. By 1700, every one of them had died. The Europeans made them work as slaves. Even worse, the newcomers carried smallpox and typhus. The native people had no immunity for these fatal diseases.

In 1655 the British invaded and ruled until 1962. Then Jamaica gained its independence. Now it governs itself. English remains the nation's official language. However, most of the people speak a dialect. A dialect has words that other English speakers do not know.

Jamaica is the third biggest island in the Caribbean Sea. It lies 90 miles south of Cuba. The land is ideal for growing sugarcane on plantations. Such huge farms need lots of manual laborers. During the 1700s Jamaica was the most important slave market in the Western Hemisphere. Over 80 percent of the people living there have a slave ancestor. Most of the people descended from Europeans, Africans, and Chinese. The Asians came to work on the plantations after slavery ended in 1838. Slavery was outlawed before that. But the slaves had to rebel to get their freedom.

Although Jamaica has many plantations, it cannot grow enough food for its people. Much of its food is imported. The plantations grow crops to export. These crops include sugarcane, citrus fruit, bananas, coffee beans, and the cacao beans used to make chocolate. Bauxite mining is one of the most important industries. This ore is used to make aluminum.

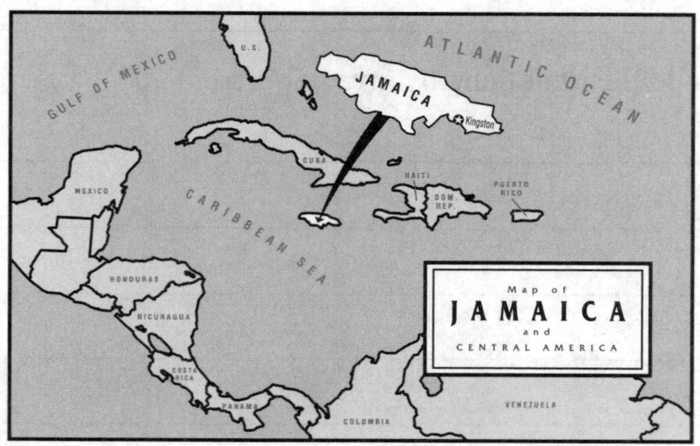

Jamaica, Jewel in the Caribbean Sea

SEE JAMAICA!

ESCAPE TO PARADISE . . . JAMAICA

Don't miss these highlights!

Our World-Famous White Sand Beaches—the island's perimeter offers endless opportunities for swimming, snorkeling, sunbathing, and relaxing.

Blue Mountains—take a hike in a national park that includes the highest peak in the nation. The beautiful Blue Mountains tower over the plains east of Kingston.

Montego Bay—one of the most famous vacation spots on Earth—and for good reason. As a marine sanctuary, you can see this underwater world in whatever way suits your fancy. You can scuba dive, snorkel, or ride in a glass-bottom boat.

The Bob Marley Museum—one of Kingston's most-visited attractions and the former home of the legendary king of reggae*, the Honourable Robert Nesta Marley.

Bamboo Rafting on the Rio Grande—relax on a rustic raft made for two as you glide down this peaceful and picturesque waterway

Dunn's River Falls—set within a small tropical rain forest, this series of waterfalls has roaring cascades, and you can swim at the base to experience the exhilaration of ice-cold spring water.

Dolphin Cove—swim and frolic with friendly bottlenose dolphins!

Steel Drum Bands—Listen and dance to the rhythm of our world-famous steel drum bands.

Appleton Estate Rum Tour—offers you the chance to participate in making rum. Visitors can juice their own sugar cane, sample white rum, and boil "wet sugar."

Entry/Exit Information: U.S. citizens must have a U.S. passport to enter Jamaica. Tourists must also have a return ticket and show sufficient funds for their visit. U.S. citizens traveling to Jamaica for work or extended stays must have a current U.S. passport and a visa issued by the Jamaican Embassy. All travelers pay a departure tax to leave the nation.

*popular form of music with a strong beat

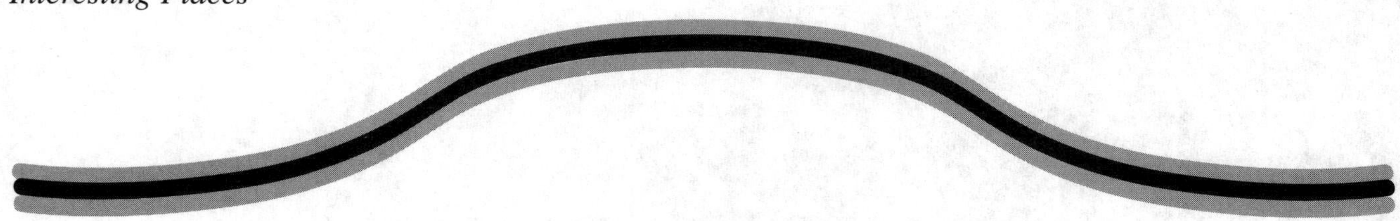

Jamaica, Jewel in the Caribbean Sea

1. Jamaica lies close to

a. Spain.

b. Great Britain.

c. Cuba.

d. China.

2. A dialect is a

a. foreign language.

b. variation of a major language.

c. language that is no longer used.

d. language made from a combination of four different languages.

3. One of Jamaica's biggest industries is

a. making medicines from tropical plants.

b. mining silver.

c. selling slaves.

d. tourism.

4. The arrival of the Spanish was beneficial for the Jamaican natives. True or False? Explain.

____

____

____

5. Why does Jamaica have entry and exit requirements for travelers?

____

____

____

____

____

6. Would you like to visit Jamaica as a tourist? Use information from the brochure to explain your stance.

____

____

____

____

____

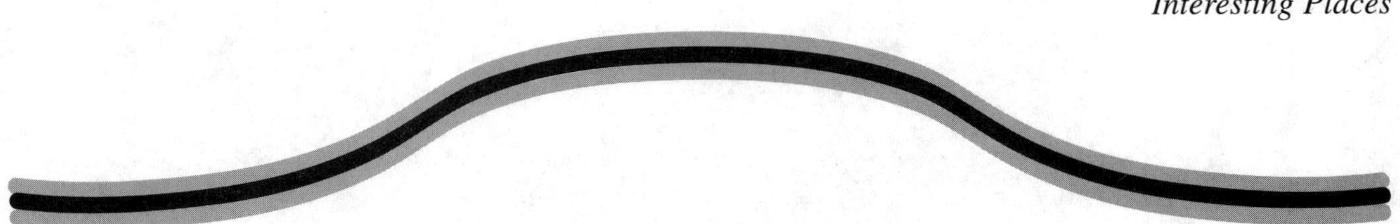

Swaziland, Land of a Single Culture

Swaziland is a tiny, landlocked nation in Africa. On a continent where water is scarce, this country is fortunate. It has four rivers to use for generating power and watering crops. The mild climate is good for growing crops. The nation has deposits of coal, gold, tin, and iron ore. Mining is an important industry.

Swaziland is also fortunate to have one culture. Most African nations have many cultures and languages. This has led to fighting and continuous civil wars. Swaziland is one of the most stable countries on the continent due to the efforts of King Mswati II. He ascended to the throne in 1840. Since the king felt it was important to unite the many tribes into one nation, he had young men of the same age brought together from different tribes to form armies. These groups became known for their military skill and discipline. The king's plan has continued. Today every young man belongs to an age group organized by the current king.

King Sobhuza II ruled from 1921 until 1982. He led his nation as it gained independence from Great Britain in 1968. The king's mother made sure he got an education. She also had a group of boys from all levels of Swazi society educated. They served as the king's advisors. They helped him to stay in touch with all of his people. Today his son rules. More than 80 percent of all adults know how to read and write.

In the early 1900s, vultures left Swaziland. Vultures eat dead animals. Their departure signaled a lack of wildlife. Over-hunting and several diseases had made Swaziland's large mammals die off. Now game* parks have been set aside and animals reintroduced. In 1987 one man paid $250,000 for a breeding group of five rhinoceroses as a gift to a park. But within four years poachers killed all of them for their horns.

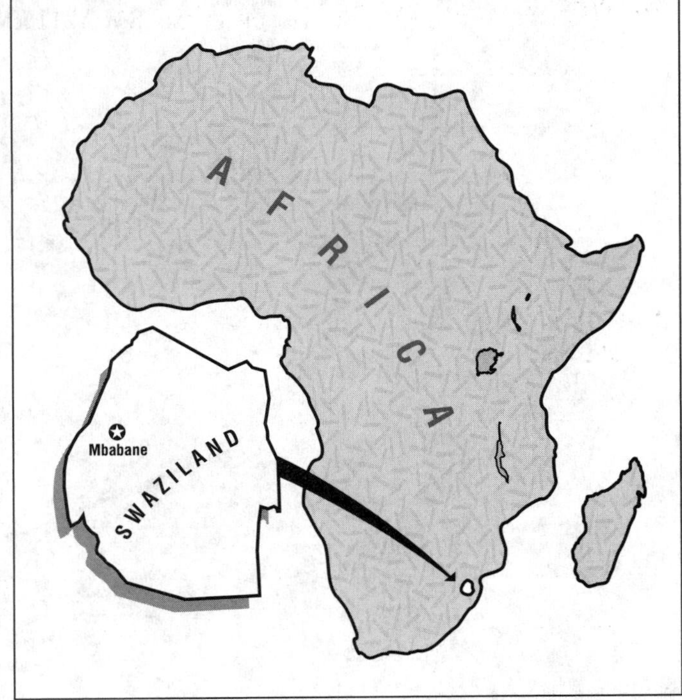

Yet Swaziland's biggest challenge is the health of its people. This nation has the world's highest rate of the deadly HIV and AIDS infection. Some estimates state that more than 40 percent of all adults are infected. This may be why Swazis also have the world's lowest life expectancy (32.5 years). Life expectancy is the age at which the average person dies.

*wildlife

Swaziland, Land of a Single Culture

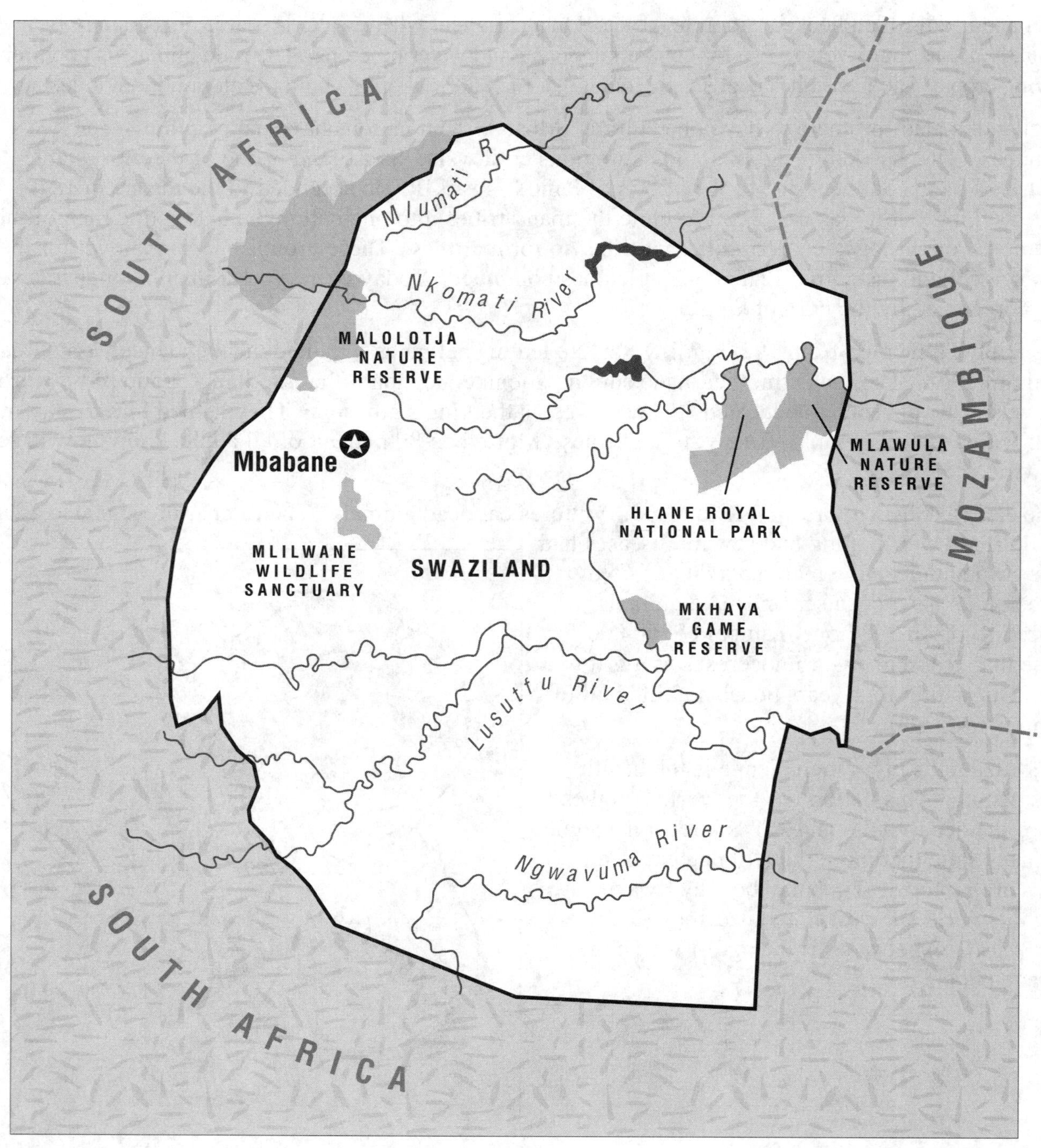

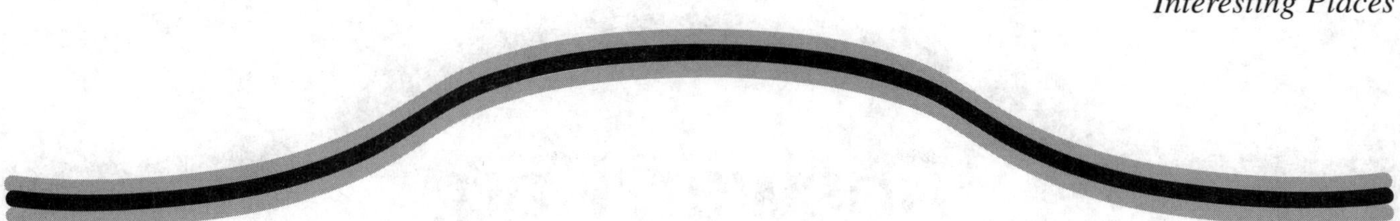

Swaziland, Land of a Single Culture

1. King Mswati II ruled Swaziland

a. hundreds of years ago.
b. during the 1800s.
c. during the 1900s.
d. for the past 50 years and still today.

2. What is an asset that Swaziland lacks?

a. healthy people
b. rivers
c. land for growing crops
d. a unified culture

3. One advantage that Swaziland has over many other African nations is

a. lots of wildlife.
b. wealthy people.
c. a long life expectancy.
d. a lack of civil wars.

4. Look at the map. The areas set aside to encourage wildlife to live in Swaziland are located in the southern part of the nation. True or False? Explain.

____

____

____

5. What are the names of Swaziland's rivers and what can you conclude about the unnamed waterways shown on the map?

____

____

____

____

____

6. Has Swaziland's government allocated enough land for wildlife? Defend your stance.

____

____

____

____

____

Answer Key

page 12

1. c 2. b 3. d

4. True. When Mount Vesuvius erupted again in 1631, about 16,500 fewer people died than in the 79 eruption.

5. In terms of deadly volcanoes, the worst nation in which to live is Indonesia. The chart shows that the number of people killed by volcanoes in that nation is 115,000!

6. Yes. The volcano could erupt again and if it does, it will kill people and destroy many homes. OR No. Today the volcano is monitored so adequate warning could be given for the people to evacuate. Now there are more ways to escape (roads and helicopters) than in 79. However, they would still lose their property.

page 15

1. b 2. d 3. a

4. False. The dead bodies in shallow graves provided more food for the rats. Burning the corpses would have been a better way to stem the spread of the disease. The flames protected Pope Clement.

5. Accurate birth and death records weren't kept at that time because few people knew how to write. So the death tolls are just estimates. Also, according to the encyclopedia entry, the Black Death swept across Europe more than once, which accounts for the differences in dates.

6. Yes. If people had known, they would have killed the rats. They would've kept their bodies and homes clean with soap and water, so the germs would not have spread as far or as fast. Cleanliness would also have cut down on the amount of the rats, too. OR No. Even if the people had kept themselves and their homes clean, the germs spread through the air when people coughed. Also, they had no good way to bury the dead bodies or dispose of sewage to curb the rat population.

page 18

1. b 2. d 3. a

4. True. The brochure indicates that by moving at a right angle to the slide, you may avoid the avalanche's fastest-moving snow.

5. Probably not. The avalanche in Yungay, Peru was not a typical avalanche. The slide contained boulders, water, mud, trees, snow, and ice. The advice given in the pamphlet is for a snow slide.

6. Yes, I think it is fair because it's the resort's policy. It is clearly stated, and the management put it in place to save lives in case of a disaster. If the person doesn't want to wear the rescue beacon, he or she should go to another ski resort that doesn't require one. OR No, I do not think it is fair because the person has paid for the lift ticket. If the person is willing to risk his or her life by not wearing a rescue beacon, then the person should sign a release stating that. Then the loved ones couldn't sue the resort if the person died in an avalanche.

page 21

1. a 2. b 3. c

4. False. The people who went to the harbor died. If they had known how bad the explosion would be, they would have run just like the crew of the *Mont Blanc*. OR False. The people were curious about the fire. They didn't understand that it would cause a deadly explosion.

5. Luc, the letter writer, was a crew member on the *Mont Blanc*. Public opinion was against the crew. People felt that they could have put out the fire if they had stayed. So Luc does not want to admit who he really is because he's afraid that no one will hire him.

6. Yes, the *Mont Blanc* crew did the right thing by leaving the ship. The fire was beyond their control. They didn't have a way to put it out, and the captain gave the order to abandon the ship. They did what anyone in their position would do and ran for their lives. OR No, the *Mont Blanc* crew did not do the right thing. If they had stayed, they could have sunk the ship and stopped the fire. That would have kept an awful tragedy from happening.

page 24

1. c 2. d 3. c

4. False. Morrison doesn't say how it got started and even today no one knows for sure what caused the fire.

5. As the *Hindenburg* is approaching the mooring mast, Morrison sounds proud and thrilled to be reporting about it. When it bursts into flames, he sounds excited and horrified. After it crashes, he has to go inside because he's so upset. He says it's the worst thing he's ever seen.

6. Yes. The American government made the right decision because the Nazi government was building up its military and did eventually declare war on America. OR No. The American government made the wrong decision because the *Hindenburg* tragedy could have been prevented if the blimp had been filled with helium instead of hydrogen. And the Nazi government, while aggressive, never used blimps in World War II.

page 27

1. a 2. d 3. c

4. False. Christa McAuliffe has only been teaching at Concord High School for 3 years. Probably teachers with more experience applied to go. NASA felt that McAuliffe was a gifted teacher and an excellent communicator.

5. Christa McAuliffe probably felt excited and proud to have been chosen from 11,500 applicants. She probably looked

Answer Key *(cont.)*

forward to the experience but knew that she would miss her husband, children, and family while she was in space.

6. Yes, NASA should allow civilians to ride the space shuttle. If civilians are made aware of the dangers and choose to go anyway, that is their right. They can choose to take the risk. OR No, NASA should not let civilians ride the space shuttle. Space travel is risky and best left to astronauts who have trained for years, know how to handle emergencies, and are willing to face the dangers.

page 30

1. d 2. c 3. b
4. True. The people did not get a warning because there are no sensors in the Indian Ocean. OR False. Even with warning, many people would have died because it happened just 155 miles offshore and raced toward the island at 500 miles per hour. There was not enough time for people to move far enough inland.
5. The second-worst tsunami was the one in Lisbon, Portugal in 1755 because 100,000 people lost their lives. It was caused by an earthquake, just like the 2004 tsunami in the Indian Ocean.
6. Yes. The Indonesian government should declare the coastal regions of Java and Sumatra uninhabitable because of the scope of the natural disasters that have occurred there. The next one is just a matter of time. So the government should make it into parkland and offer the people land elsewhere. OR No. The Indonesian government should not declare the coastal regions of Java and Sumatra uninhabitable. After all, there are natural dangers in many settings. People are not told they can't live where there are numerous earthquakes, tornadoes, or volcanoes.

page 33

1. b 2. c 3. a
4. True. Before 1787 the system had been tried in England but had failed. The meeting minutes of the Philadelphia Society for Alleviating the Miseries of Public Prisons show that the Society was aware of this fact. But the members thought that they could improve the system and make it work in America.
5. The meeting minutes describe prisoners starving to death unless fed by compassionate people. They also mention people being naked and getting frostbite because they had to give their clothing to the guards in order to get food. This indicates corruption on the part of the guards.
6. Yes, the Pennsylvania System would have worked if the inmates had been allowed some social interaction. For many of the people, the prison was the best living conditions they had ever had. And they learned a useful skill. But the silence and isolation was unbearable. OR No, even if the inmates had been allowed daily interaction with each other, the Pennsylvania System was doomed. Living alone was too costly for the taxpayers to tolerate.

page 36

1. d 2. a 3. c
4. False. The chickens provided eggs, and the goats provided milk.
5. Yeoman Safford writes that the blockade runners didn't know their ship was in the area. It appears that a false rumor had been spread saying their ship was in Europe. Therefore, Captain Stellwagen thought that the blockade runners would not have their guard up or be suspicious if the *USS Constellation* approached them.
6. Yes, it was fair. In order to maintain discipline, it is essential that an obvious division be established between the officers and the crew. Part of that separation is the improved living conditions of the officers. OR No, it was not fair. The captain and officers should have shared the good food with the sailors in order to keep up their strength and prevent illness. Crews would still respect leaders who endured the same conditions as they did.

page 39

1. b 2. d 3. d
4. True. Once the ship reached its destination, it might have been hard for Captain Kendall to keep Crippen on board. Once off the ship, he could have disappeared into the crowd. By radioing ahead, the police were ready to board the ship as soon as it docked. Crippen was trapped on board.
5. Since she was trying to disguise herself as a teenage boy, it showed that she must have realized that they were hiding from the police. She was helping Crippen get away, so she was an accomplice.
6. Yes, the U.S. government should regulate the language and music broadcast via radio because people shouldn't hear bad language and music that encourages drug use or violence. OR No, the U.S. government should not regulate the language and music broadcast via radio because that of the freedom of speech guaranteed by the Constitution. If people don't like the language and music they hear, they can change the station or turn off the radio.

page 42

1. d 2. b 3. c
4. False. According to the sales flyer in 1912 a Ford Model T Touring Car cost $690. OR False. According to the sales flyer in 1912 a Ford Model T Town Car cost $900.
5. The sales flyer emphasizes the high quality and reliability of the Ford Model T. It also points out the Model T's popularity by stating that it's the best-known car on Earth and that 1/3 of all cars sold in the U.S. that year will be Fords. The sales flyer mentions that the prices of the cars

Answer Key (cont.)

have dropped, indicating that they are a good value. It also states that every car is well equipped and perhaps the competitors' cars aren't. (Accept any three of the details highlighted)

6. Yes, by dropping prices, more people could afford a car than ever before. This led to such steady sales that Ford sold one out of every three cars in America by 1912. OR No. The Ford Motor Company should not have lowered its prices so that it could have kept more of the profits.

page 45

1. d 2. c 3. a
4. True. The March 1932 poster about his missing child says that the baby was kidnapped from his home in Hopewell, New Jersey. Charles Lindbergh lived there with his son.
5. The kidnappers believed that Charles Lindbergh was rich because he had won $25,000 for his transatlantic flight. He also had enough money to turn down multiple moneymaking opportunities which were offered to him.
6. No, Charles Lindbergh did the right thing by paying the kidnappers. He thought that it was his only chance of saving his child and had no idea that they would kill his son in spite of the money. Yes, Charles Lindbergh made a mistake by paying the kidnappers. They had no reason to keep his son alive once they received the money. He should have kept stalling until the police could locate his child.

page 48

1. a 2. d 3. d
4. False. The moon's gravity is weaker than Earth's. OR False. The Earth's gravity is stronger than the moon's.
5. Hannamaker, the letter writer, has two main criticisms of the *Apollo 11* mission. Her first is that the money for the space program could have been better spent on aid for the poor. Her second is that there are no practical benefits to having put men on the moon and that it was just done to make U.S. citizens feel proud of the nation.
6. I agree with the letter writer that going to the moon was an extravagant waste of money. The funds could've been put to much better use here on Earth. Perhaps by now we could've eliminated starvation or disease in underdeveloped nations with the money that was spent going to the moon. OR No, I disagree with the letter writer. The scientific knowledge gained by developing spacecraft and visiting the moon made the expense worthwhile.

page 51

1. c 2. a 3. d
4. False. Neither of the Rosenbergs were convicted of treason. They were convicted of conspiracy.
5. The statements that appeal to the reader's emotions are: "Rosenbergs' Wedding Anniversary Set as their Execution Date"; "Two Young Sons Will Become Orphans"; "They were convicted by the testimony of liars!"; "You and your buddies fought and died for the freedoms and rights of all American citizens."; "Don't let this travesty of justice occur!" (accept any two). The poster uses emotional statements to get people to act. People are more apt to take action based on feelings of fear, outrage, or anger than for logical, rational reasons.
6. Neither of the Rosenbergs should have been executed because they were never tried or found guilty of treason; I don't believe in the death penalty; I don't think they were guilty, etc. OR Just Julius should have been executed because there was evidence against him (telegrams) and Alexsandr Feklisov admits he was a spy. There was no real evidence against Ethel! Also, it is not a crime to know that your spouse is doing something illegal and not turn him in. OR Both of the Rosenbergs should have been executed because Julius betrayed his country by meeting with Alexsandr Feklisov and giving him a document and Ethel betrayed her country by knowing what her husband was doing but failing to stop or report him.

page 54

1. c 2. d 3. b
4. True. Sallie died at Gravelly Run. The monument indicates that the regiment later fought at Five Forks and Appomattox.
5. A casualty of this regiment was most apt to be wounded, as 772 of the 1,432 total casualties were injured. A total of 402 men died and another 258 went missing.
6. Yes, the policy was wise because the risk of a terrorist infecting a stray animal with a fatal disease or blowing up the animal once it was inside the camp was just too great. OR No, the policy was not wise because the troops could have received the same benefits from having mascots just as troops in former wars did. Also, it was cruel to tell the troops they had to shoot stray animals since most Americans like dogs and cats, and it is illegal to shoot them at home.

page 57

1. a 2. c 3. d
4. False. The Asian carp were deliberately brought to Arkansas ponds and now people are trying to keep them from spreading into the Great Lakes. OR False. The zebra mussel was brought into the Great Lakes accidentally, but the Asian carp was brought in on purpose to clean up water in Arkansas. The Asian carp has not yet invaded the Great Lakes and efforts are being made to keep them out.

Answer Key *(cont.)*

5. The three major problems caused by the zebra mussels in the Great Lakes are making the water so clear so that fish get skin cancer, making the water more acidic, and eating all the algae the native fish needed. As a result of these problems, some native fish species have vanished.
6. Yes, having monetary penalties would make people less likely to bring in foreign species or release pets into the wild. Both actions can have catastrophic effects on the environment, many of which may not even be able to be anticipated. OR No, having monetary penalties would not stop people from importing exotic animals or releasing their pets into the wild. Too few people would actually be caught. Only educating people about the dangers of such behaviors will have a significant impact on the problem.

page 60

1. d 2. a 3. b

4. False. Now women as well as men are recruited into the U.S. Coast Guard. Also, there is no longer a need for coal heavers. The enlistment length and benefits may have changed, too. (Give credit for any of these ideas.)
5. Yes, the ad would have attracted many applicants. At that time many people worked long hours for low pay. There were a lot of sweatshop jobs, too. The ad promises good pay, medical care, and an amazing retirement plan at 3/4 pay. As a result, many men would have liked to have joined the U.S. Coast Guard in 1917.
6. Yes, I think that being a part of the U.S. Coast Guard would be an exciting career. Protecting America's coastline, stopping illegal drugs and immigrants, and saving and rescuing people at sea are important jobs. If the benefits are like those of 1917, it would be a financially good idea, too, etc. OR No, I would not like to join the U.S. Coast Guard because I am afraid of water, don't know how to swim, don't want to be a part of the military, do not think the jobs sound interesting, etc. (Allow responses that are supported and explained.)

page 63

1. d 2. c 3. b

4. False. From 1886–1947 a law removed the president pro tempore from the line of presidential succession.
5. It is essential to have a clear line of succession for the U.S. presidency because if both the president and vice president are killed, someone needs to take charge immediately. Having a line of succession in writing prevents arguments and confusion, letting the appropriate person take control of the nation.
6. The current line of succession is better than prior ones because it puts elected officials ahead of appointed ones (such as the Secretary of State and cabinet members). Elected officials have been chosen by the people. OR The current line of succession is worse than prior ones because it used to go directly to cabinet members after the vice president. Cabinet members meet daily with the U.S. president. This means that at any given moment Cabinet members are the most up-to-date on the national and world situation. They would make a smoother transition than the Speaker or the president pro tempore.

page 66

1. c 2. d 3. a

4. True. Steel roller coasters allow for more daring designs. As a result, steel coasters could do things—such as inverted loops and have riders stand up—that wooden coasters could not do. This brought about a new roller coaster craze.
5. The designers know that people want roller coasters that are scary. The people who made the Komodo wanted potential riders to think of one of the world's scariest creatures. So the sneak preview ticket emphasizes how terrifying the real komodo dragon is and compares it to the roller coaster.
6. Yes. I'd like to ride the Komodo because I love roller coasters. I like the speed, flipping upside down, and dropping sensations. I'm willing to try anything once. OR No, I would not ride the Komodo because I'm afraid of roller coasters; don't like heights, have motion sickness, faint or throw up on roller coasters; don't like the feeling of dropping. (Allow any reasonable responses.)

page 69

1. b 2. a 3. d

4. True. Dix states that the mentally ill are kept chained in filth—often in damp and dark dungeons. She states that they "suffer indescribable pains and abuses." She says that she's seen the insane subjected to every sort of cruelty, neglect, and ill management.
5. Dix wants the General Government (federal government) to provide the funds to assist the states' reform and to help build adequate facilities for the mentally ill.
6. Yes. Most people do not want to admit they have mental illness even today because they are afraid that people will reject them. People are more likely to reveal the fact that they have a physical illness because it's more acceptable. Also, many people still believe that mental illness is just mental weakness—and that the insane could "just snap out of it" if they'd make an effort. OR No. Today there is a greater stigma in having some physical illnesses (such as AIDS) than there is in having a mental illness. More people are starting to understand and accept mental illness than ever before.

Answer Key (cont.)

page 72

1. c   2. b   3. d
4. False. Edison was a millionaire long before he invented the concrete homes. OR False. Since Edison was already a millionaire, he never intended to make a profit on the concrete homes and felt that he was doing it to improve conditions for the poor.
5. Edison's houses probably never became popular because concrete can crack and leak. Also, it is hard to work on electrical lines and plumbing behind concrete walls. People like homes they can easily change and add onto, which was hard if not impossible with a concrete home. The poor for whom he had designed the houses couldn't afford a piece of land to put the house on and richer people didn't want others to think they were so poor they had to have a concrete house. Edison's houses might have sold better if he had not emphasized that they were designed for the poor. (Accept any two of the reasons highlighted.)
6. Yes, concrete houses would succeed today because now people willingly live in mobile homes, modular homes, and condominiums. So they would be more accepting of a concrete house, especially if it were inexpensive. OR No, concrete houses wouldn't succeed today, either. The factors that kept them from being popular the first time still apply.

page 75

1. a   2. c   3. b
4. False. Gandhi reaffirmed his belief in nonviolence by fasting after the massacre and telling his followers not to bring about more bloodshed. OR False. Gandhi never changed his stance on nonviolence and reaffirmed his belief in it during a speech before the All-India Congress in 1942.
5. From Gandhi's speech, it is clear that the Indian nationalists had been in favor of a revolt against the British since the British were occupied in fighting to keep their own nation from being invaded.
6. Yes, the world would be a better place if today's world leaders followed Gandhi's nonviolent policies. A nonviolent answer can always be found to any problem. Some of the greatest social changes have occurred as a result of peaceful protests of Mohandas Gandhi and Martin Luther King, Jr. OR No, the world would not be a better place if today's world leaders followed Gandhi's nonviolent policies. There are some instances in which one must fight to defend one's nation. Dealing with terrorists in a nonviolent fashion simply does not work. Nonviolent protests work to bring about social change but they do not work against invading armies or terrorism.

page 78

1. d   2. c   3. b
4. True. Many parents did not want to let their children go. They were not sure that the children were in danger and thought that they could do the best job protecting them. OR False. The hardest part was getting the kids out of the Ghetto safely without the Gestapo discovering what was going on.
5. Marta's letter to Irena has a tone that is both grateful and sad. She is writing to thank Irena for saving her life. She says "thank you" multiple times and calls Irena brave. Yet Marta is sad because she lost her entire family and her religion in being adopted by a Christian/Catholic family. While she wants Irena to know that she's grateful, it's hard for Marta not to show the depth of her sorrow.
6. Yes, I would have joined Zegota. The members of that group were courageous and fought against a great evil. I would have been proud to have been one of them. OR No, I would not have joined Zegota. I would have been too afraid of the Nazis and getting caught and being tortured as Irena was. I am not as brave as Irena Sendler. OR I do not know for sure what I would have done in that situation. I'd like to say that I would have joined Zegota, but when I look at the statistics and see that more than half of all European Jews were killed, it becomes clear that few people actually had the courage to join rescue groups.

page 81

1. b   2. a   3. c
4. False. He wrote a dissenting (disagreeing) opinion to state that he did not agree with the Court's ruling. He felt that quotas at universities would help to undo years of damage and hardship that minorities had faced in American education.
5. An affirmative action program is one that seeks to give minorities better access to educational admission and employment opportunities. Often this includes quotas to make schools or employers select a specific number of minority applicants. The goal is to have a more diverse student and professional population. (Give credit if students talk about affirmative action in education or employment.)
6. Yes. Affirmative action programs are necessary to overcome prejudice against minorities in order to "level the playing field." Without affirmative action programs, minorities would not have made the advances in higher education and professional careers that they have. OR No. Affirmative action programs discriminate against white applicants and insult minorities by implying that they cannot compete for admissions or employment based

Answer Key *(cont.)*

on their grades and work performance. (Give credit if students talk about affirmative action in education or employment.)

page 84

1. c
2. a
3. d
4. True. Mother Teresa was impressed by the attitude of the dying people she had met. In her Nobel Peace Prize acceptance speech, she talks about how amazing they are. She tells the story of two of them and how they did not complain about their misfortunes but instead showed her gratitude.
5. Mother Teresa talked about the people that she met in her daily life because she wanted others to know how wonderful the people she worked with are. She wanted to make them real and compelling to the listeners. We hear of hundreds dying each day on the streets, but we cannot imagine it. She wanted us to know that the people are just like us, only unfortunate.
6. I thought that the dying woman who said thank you and died was the most moving story because she did not complain or wail, "Why me?" Instead she was grateful to die in a bed rather than on a street. OR I thought that the dying man who said that he was going to die like an angel was the most moving story. He did not complain, curse anyone, or make comparisons. Instead he showed actual joy that he was going to die in better conditions than he had lived! OR I thought that the little boy who brought his sugar to Mother Teresa for her children was the most moving story because he showed the incredible power Mother Teresa had—the power to make others care about those in need. The child knew what she was doing and wanted to help her, even in a small way.

page 87

1. a
2. b
3. c
4. True. The two groups also agree that the Quran is the holy book, that Allah will resurrect all people and question them, and that it is wrong to make images of Allah or humans.
5. The two differences in beliefs that probably cause the strongest disagreements between the Sunnis and the Shiites is their view of women and their idea of Allah being able to command people to commit evil acts, which then makes the acts just. (You can accept any two of the differences listed between the two sects as long as a logical reason is provided.)
6. Yes, if Afghanistan did not have a state religion, fighting would decrease between the Sunnis and Shiites. Other religions might spring up in the nation and give the Muslims a common enemy. OR No, even if Afghanistan did not have a state religion, it would have no effect on the different interpretations of Islam that cause the fighting between the Sunnis and Shiites. Most of the people in that nation are Muslims, and there has been fighting between them for years.

page 90

1. d
2. a
3. b
4. False. The Arctic Circle does not get as cold as Antarctica because it is surrounded by continents that give off heat. OR False. Antarctica is colder than the Arctic Circle because it is surrounded by icy ocean water instead of land.
5. Yes, Robert Scott is impressed with the way that Titus Oates met his death. In his journal, he calls Oates "a brave soul" and says that the has borne intense suffering without complaint.
6. Yes, if the men had tried to hike the 11 miles to the depot, they would have had a better chance of surviving. Amundsen and his team survived a four-day blizzard. Instead Scott's team kept waiting for the storm to break until they ran out of fuel and food and were too weak to move. OR No, if the men had tried to hike the 11 miles to the depot, they would most probably have died anyway. They would've gotten too cold from the windchill and with all the snow in the air they might not have been able to find their way to the depot. Also, how could they know that the gale and swirling snow would not let up for many days? They kept hoping that if they waited just a little longer that the storm would break.

page 93

1. b
2. d
3. a
4. True. The only continent that gets less rainfall than Australia is Antarctica. OR True. Australia gets less rainfall than Africa, Europe, Asia, North America, or South America.
5. There are four possible reasons for the lack of trees on Kangaroo Island. The first is that the fungus Phytophthera is killing off the trees. The second is that the koalas are eating too many of the trees' leaves, which kills the trees. Wildfires burn many trees. And sheep and wild pigs eating most of the new tree sprouts.
6. The baby koalas on Kangaroo Island need to be spayed or neutered to reduce the koala population to a level the island can support. OR Some of the koalas on Kangaroo Island should be moved to the mainland. OR Some of the koalas on Kangaroo Island should be sold to zoos. OR The weakest koalas on Kangaroo Island should be found and killed (humanely) so that the strongest ones can survive. (Accept any of the solutions offered in the article, a combination of solutions, or reasonable student-proposed ideas that reduce the number of koalas.)

Answer Key (cont.)

page 96

1. c 2. d 3. b
4. True. Bulgaria is a developing nation because it was economically damaged by Communism. Wages are low, but the cost of necessities are high. Bulgarians have one of the lowest standards of living in Europe.
5. The purpose of Adolf Beckerle's telegram to Nazi headquarters was to warn the leadership that the Bulgarians had positive feelings toward their Jewish population. He indicated that the Bulgarians may not cooperate in the deportation of their Jews.
6. Yes, I think that Bulgaria's policies about high school are wise because not all students want to go to college or are capable of earning a college degree. Having vocational high schools lets students who are struggling with traditional education get valuable job skills so they can get a job upon graduation. By the time a student is choosing a high school, it's pretty clear whether a trade or a college degree is in their future. OR No, I do not think that Bulgaria's policies about high school are wise because it is too limiting. People grow and change even as adults. Students might not take school seriously when they are young but then want to get a college education when they are adults. But if they went to a vocational high school, the doors to college are forever closed for them. The current policy forces people to make a really big life decision when they are still teenagers.

page 99

1. d 2. a 3. d
4. True. In fact, the Great Mosque in Samarra, Iraq, is a good example of Islamic architecture. It is a minaret, which is commonly used in Islamic architecture.
5. The Great Mosque, a place of prayer, was built more than 1,100 years ago. At that time it was the largest one on Earth. It tells us that Iraqis of the past valued Islam because they had to work for 30 years to build the mosque.
6. Yes, the United States did the right thing by invading Iraq in 2003 because Hussein was a dangerous leader who had to be removed from power. Most of the Iraqis were relieved to be out from under his control. And if Iraq can become a successful democracy, then it will help to stabilize the troubled Middle East. OR No, the United States did not do the right thing by invading Iraq in 2003 because there was no clear evidence that the leader had weapons of mass destruction or was harboring members of al-Qaeda. The war in Iraq destabilized the troubled Middle East. It also made more terrorists want to target the United States.

page 102

1. c 2. b 3. d
4. False. The arrival of the Spanish was a disaster for the Jamaican natives. The Spanish enslaved the people. They also carried sicknesses for which the Jamaicans had no immunity. About 200 years after the Spanish arrived, every native was dead!
5. Jamaica has entry requirements that make tourists show that they have a return ticket and enough money to last for their visit. They do not want people to go there and then never leave. They want people to come as tourists, not immigrants. All travelers must pay a departure tax. The Jamaican government probably uses these funds to improve the country (maintain roads, provide medical care for the poor, etc.). Since this tax did not put a damper on tourism, it's a great way to bring money into the nation.
6. Yes, I would like to visit Jamaica as a tourist. I love doing things outdoors and hiking in the mountains, swimming with dolphins and looking at coral reefs sound like great fun. I'd enjoy the white sand beaches and sunbathing. Playing in waterfalls, rafting on a river, and making rum would be great, too. I like reggae and would love to hear a steel drum and, etc. OR No, I would not like to visit Jamaica because I don't really like doing things outdoors. Most of the activities in the brochure were swimming, hiking, diving, and rafting. I prefer going to a city on vacation so I can visit museums and the theater. (As long as the student uses information from the brochure in the answer, allow any combination of reasons.)

page 105

1. b 2. a 3. d
4. False. There are four nature/game reserves, and they are all in the northern part of Swaziland.
5. There are four main rivers. They are the Mlumati, Nkomati, Lusutfu, and Ngwavuma. The remaining waterways are smaller, like streams. They are distributed all over the country which allows irrigation for farming.
6. Yes. The nation is small, but it has four wildlife reserves. After nearly all wildlife was eliminated in the 19th century, species are being reintroduced into these areas. OR No. The nation has no wildlife reserves in the southern portion of the country, and the ones in the north are small. Since most of the wildlife died out in the 19th century, the nation should set aside more areas to promote successful reintroduction of native animals.